Devon Rex Cats

This publication is Copyright 2014 by EKL Publishing. All products, publications, software and services mentioned and recommended in this publication are protected by trademarks. In such instance, all trademarks & copyright belong to the respective owners.

The moral rights of the author has been asserted
British Library Cataloguing in Publication Data
A catalogue record for this book is available from the British Library

ISBN 978-1-909820-69-2

Disclaimer and Legal Notice

Devon Rex Cats

The Pet Owner's Guide to Devon Rex Cats and Kittens

Including Buying, Daily Care, Personality, Temperament, Health, Diet and Breeders

Colette Anderson

Foreword

My interest in cats with curly or "rex" coats actually began with the Cornish Rex and then extended to the Devon Rex. Genetically, they are a fascinating pair, each originating from a unique mutation. If you mate the two breeds, the kittens have straight coats. Although veritable next door neighbors in the United Kingdom where they originated, these are separate and special breeds.

Of the two, the Devon Rex is arguably the real "odd ball." Early in my research I read that the best way to "meet" the Devon Rex was to throw away every preconceived notion about what a cat *should* look like. It's good advice. Alternately described as elfin, pixyish, and alien, a Devon can take a little getting used to.

But once you get past the exaggerated features and unusual coat, and really spend some time with a Devon, you realize you're in the presence of a powerhouse personality. My first real encounter with the breed's larger than life way of being in the world involved a granola muffin.

I wanted to meet a Devon Rex, so my vet put me in contact with a local woman who raised the cats. She graciously invited me to her home for tea and a chance to spend some time with her Devons.

After the initial introductions, my hostess brought out a lovely tea service and a plate of warm granola muffins she'd just taken out of the oven. I reached for one, looking forward to biting into the freshly baked pastry when I was essentially mugged by one of the cats.

The furry felon launched himself into one of the most well executed horizontal dives I've ever seen, sailed past my nose, nabbed the muffin in mid-air and landed on the other side of the couch, swallowing his purloined treat before anyone could react.

My bemused new friend laughed and said, "Well, you said you wanted to meet a Devon Rex. Now you have."

The famously prodigious Devon appetite is not confined to begging. They can and will resort to outright thievery in pursuit of a treat. I have since learned to guard my plate when in the presence of these cats and to ignore their doleful pleasing stares.

Within fifteen minutes, this same cat proceeded to launch himself onto my shoulder when I stood up from the couch to take a tour of the cattery. He rode there the entire time I walked around, offering gentle color commentary in my ear with a series of chirps and mews. I was in love.

Historically, the big cat breeds have been my favorites, but I also like cats with an advisory frame of mind. I like my feline companions to be present and interactive. That's the Devon Rex and then some. I would not recommend this breed for anyone who is away from home for an extended period of time.

Devons don't just have separation anxiety; they have separation misery. Since I work from home, my Devon is perfectly happy with the situation and gets along beautifully with my other cats. Their agreeable nature doesn't just stop with humans. Devons get along well with other animals – even the ones some cats would regard as potential snacks, although I don't take any risks.

I wish I could give you the kind of introduction to the breed that I received, but alas, you can't pack a "muffin-napping" into the pages of a book. But I can assure you, that after learning about the breed and visiting some catteries on your own, you're probably not going to be able to say no to a Devon Rex. They're one of the most fascinating breeds I've run across in 40 years of being a dedicated cat lover.

Acknowledgments

To my wonderful husband Nick, again thank you for all your assistance in helping me research and undertaking the dreaded proof reading. His observations and comments are as always invaluable and without his encouragement I would no doubt have given up on this venture a long time ago.

Just a note to say that I have written this book using American spelling as that is what I'm used to. I have given measurements in both feet and inches/pounds and ounces and also in metric. I have also given costs in US$ and GBP. Both the measurements and costs are approximate guides. I have done my best to ensure the accuracy of the information in this book as at the time of publication.

Table of Contents

Chapter 1 – Introduction

There is nothing standard or "ordinary" about the Devon Rex. It's not just his curly coat that stands out. There is a decidedly otherworldly quality about a Devon, with his rounded features, enormous ears and luminous eyes.

Standing with the sturdy confidence of a feline bulldog, Devons are energetic, engaging, and oddly elegant. If you become a Devon owner, the one question you'll be answering over and over again is, "What kind of cat is *that?*"

History of the Devon Rex Breed

The Devon Rex breed started with one amorous and elusive stray tom living around an abandoned tin mine in Buckfastleigh in Devonshire. He attracted the attention of local woman Beryl Cox who noticed his oddly curly coat. Cox tried to catch the cat, but he evaded her attempts.

Fortune smiled on Cox, however, when she befriended a tortoiseshell and white female that produced a litter of kittens by the notorious playboy in 1960.

The kittens were born near Cox's property and she was able to see that one had a curly coat like his father. She raised the little male, naming him Kirlee. From his humble origins in that field, he became the founding father of his breed.

Cox was aware of the birth of a curly-coated cat ten years earlier, Kallibunker, from whom the Cornish Rex was being cultivated. She contacted the breeders working on the line. They took Kirlee and mated him with females descended from Kallibunker.

All of the kittens were born with straight coats. The recessive genes responsible for the curly coats were not the same. Breeders referred to the genetic variation that produced the Cornish Rex as "Gene I Rex," and to that responsible for the cats now called Devon Rex as "Gene II Rex."

One of the breeders involved in the attempted mating with Kallibunker's descendants, Mrs. P. Hughes, took one of the straight-coated kittens, Golden Rain, and bred her back to Kirlee. That pairing produced two kittens with straight coats and one curly female, setting the stage for the further evolution of the Devon Rex breed.

Interestingly enough, Golden Rain was later mated to a cat with the Gene I (Cornish) Rex mutation and that litter included 2 kittens with straight coats and 2 with curly coats. This made Golden Rain the first known hybrid to carry both rex genes.

Cornish and Devon Rex Compared

The Cornish Rex coat is short, with no outer guard hairs present. The curls lie in silken, orderly rows that are exquisitely soft to the touch. The Devon coat has the typical three types of hair: guard, awn, and down. The coat is denser and more relaxed, tending to lie in billowing waves and loose curls.

The head of a Cornish Rex is egg-shaped, narrowing at the nose whereas the Devon's head is short and square with a whisker "pinch." Their noses turn slightly upwards, while the Cornish Rex has a decidedly straight Roman nose.

Both types have enormous ears, but on the Cornish Rex they are high on the top of the head. The Devon ears are lower and extend to the side. Both cats have short, curly whiskers, but the Devon's are so compact they almost seem to be absent completely.

The thin, svelte Cornish Rex has the look of a Greyhound, while the Devon is a full-bodied cat with no arch in his back or pronounced "tuck up" at the waist. Devons are broad chested with a wide "bulldog" stance thanks to front legs that come well off the shoulder.

Both breeds are highly people oriented, displaying great loyalty and affection toward their humans. They do not like to be left alone for long periods of time, and are talkative and expressive with their opinions and advice.

Physical Characteristics

Clearly from the comparison above, both the Cornish Rex and the Devon Rex are unique, but the Devon is far and away the more eye-catching and even "alien" of the two.

Known as the "pixie" of the cat world, there is something beguilingly elfin about these cats with their enormous luminous eyes and massive ears. Full whisker pads accentuate the narrow chin and prominent cheekbones, giving the Devon Rex chiseled and highly defined facial features.

They are medium in size, 6 - 9 lbs. / 2.72 - 4.08 kg compact and muscular with a slender build. Their long legs, set wide on the shoulders are slightly bowed in the front, reminiscent of a Boxer or Bulldog. Although their feet are small, the toes are very large, enhancing the Devon Rex's ability to use their paws like hands, even picking up objects.

Coat and Color

These cats are often called "feline poodles" for their silky, rippling coats. The sparse guard hairs are fragile, however, and do tend to break, so the bare minimum of grooming is recommended to avoid temporary bald patches. Don't worry though, as the hair does grow back in such cases.

In some instances a Devon will have a very sparse "suede coat," with longer hair present on the tail, legs, thighs, and ears. The effect is like the worst case of "bed head" you can imagine.

At about eight weeks of age, the coat of some Devon Rex kittens thins out or "molts" to this suede-like, "peach fuzz" quality. In these individuals, the adult coat may not come in for as long as 2 years. This isn't so bad considering the breed's expected lifespan is 9-15 years.

Like their cousins the Cornish Rex, Devons are "heat seeking" cats. They are very warm to the touch. Their body temperature of 102 F / 38.89 C is slightly higher than that of most other cats which ranges from 99.5 F to 102.5 F / 37.50 - 39.17 C. As a result, Devons love warm spots, especially in cold weather, from your lap to a position right on top of the nearest heating vent.

All solid colors, patterns, and markings are acceptable for a Devon Rex's coat, including color pointing and calico. Eye color is open, which simply means all eye colors are a possibility, with odd-eyed colors (usually blue and amber/brown) common with white coats.

To get a real sense of what is meant by "all solid colors, patterns, and markings are acceptable" go to Chapter 8 and look at the descriptions in the CFA breed standard. It will give you an idea of the immense and delightful variety found in the Devon Rex breed.

It is important to understand that the Devon Rex is *NOT* hypoallergenic. The adverse reaction in sensitive individuals is triggered by a protein deposited on the hair during self-grooming that flakes off as dander. It is this substance, Fel d 1, that triggers an allergic attack, not the hair itself. The Devon Rex does shed very little, however, and is better tolerated by those with a known cat allergy.

The Personality of the Devon Rex

The impish looks of the Devon Rex visually betray the true personality of this madcap cat whose agility extends both to his body and his mind. Friendly, lively and endlessly playful, the Devon is a wonderful family cat and companion. Many owners will assure you with complete certainty that there *has* to be monkey blood in there somewhere!

The Devon Rex is so social you may have difficulty believing you're dealing with a cat. They will quite happily learn tricks, and then come up with a variation on the routine and turn around and teach it to you. Games of tag and fetch can go on seemingly for hours, and many will even agreeably walk on a leash.

They are loyal and so intensely devoted they frequently vault up on their human's shoulders and contentedly ride around supervising whatever you happen to be doing. The running commentary is a lovely combination of trills, chirps and coos, all delivered in a gentle and genuinely interested tone of voice.

Expect a Devon to follow you around the house, jump into your lap the instant you sit down, and crawl right under the covers when it's bedtime. Their kitten-like ways are there for life, and they tend to get on very well with other animals.

This is NOT a breed that likes to be left alone for long periods of time. They don't just want companionship; they need it. This is a *serious* consideration for anyone contemplating an adoption.

Also, they are accomplished beggars, capable of convincing you with piteous wails and longing looks that they are literally starving to death. They will steal from your plate when you're not looking and you'll never find a Devon Rex who will turn down a meal at any time of the day or night.

Male or Female?

The "male or female" question is fairly standard, but with most breeds, in my experience it just doesn't make that much difference.

In general, however, I tend to take cats on an individual basis and to consider the factor of environment in the development of temperament.

I've always had male cats irrespective of breed because they are typically larger and I like big cats. This is certainly true of the Devon Rex. They are all lovely, social cats, but the males will be slightly physically larger.

I do agree with the statement that most neutered males turn into lovable lugs as soon as the excess testosterone is out of their system, but Devon Rex toms pretty much start out that way.

Some people shy away from owning male cats due to the potential for urine spraying, but I don't see this as a problem. I have never had a tom that sprayed in the house. The behavior is extremely rare with neutered males and has been, in my opinion, blown out of proportion.

More Than One?

I am personally a big advocate of adopting littermates.
Obviously with a pedigreed breed like the Devon Rex, this
can be expensive, but the long-term benefits are
considerable. The special bond that siblings enjoy seems to
keep the animals more kittenish and playful as they age,
but even single Devon Rex cats retain these qualities
throughout their lives.

I've lived with two Russian Blue males, brothers, for a
number of years and they wrestle just as vigorously at ten
years of age as they did when they were gawky
adolescents. They're wonderful company for one another
when I'm away, and definitely double trouble when it
comes to thinking up creative things to get into.

I wouldn't discourage anyone from owning two cats of any kind, but you must understand that the Devon Rex really does need to live in a home where he's going to get lots of love, attention and interaction. While two Devons will keep each other company up to a point, then they'll just be neurotically lonely together.

The breed does extremely well with other pets, which can mitigate their high requirement for company, but seriously consider how many feline masters you want to serve before adopting the second Devon Rex. They will get on brilliantly together, but the real question is, are *you* up for it?

With Children

The Devon Rex is a fine companion for a child, but I always say that with a very firm caveat – make sure you teach your children how to be kind and respectful to ALL animals.

When a child comes away from an encounter with a cat sporting a scratch, I'm afraid my first question is usually, "What did you do to the cat?" Any animal that is being harassed, handled roughly, or actually hurt can hardly be blamed for reacting. Within this understanding, however, you should see very positive interactions with Devons and children.

With Other Pets

The Devon Rex is a truly social cat who does extremely well with others of their own kind, cats in general, dogs, and even pets other felines would see as snacks, like birds and rabbits.

I do recommend a tight lid on the fish tank, hamster habitat or other pet enclosure, but typically you won't have to worry about a Devon turning into a marauder. They just like "folks" regardless of the species.

Hypoallergenic?

There really is no such thing as a hypoallergenic cat. The negative reaction does not come from the animal's cast off hair, but rather from a protein (Fel d 1) in a cat's saliva that transfers to the fur during grooming and is scattered through dried flakes.

That being said, people with a known cat allergy do tend to tolerate the Devon Rex better than other cat breeds, but there is no guarantee that this will be the case. Do not believe any breeder who tells you any cat is truly hypoallergenic.

Inside or Out?

The Devon Rex is definitely an indoor cat. Their curly coat does not provide them with ample protection against sunburn for long periods of time, and they are far too trusting for their own good. Beyond that, in simple, practical terms, a pedigreed cat like a Devon Rex is an expensive investment.

Frankly, I do not believe any cat, including the very hardy Domestic Shorthair, often referred to as an "alley cat," should be allowed outside.

My cats have been exclusively indoor pets for the more than 40 years that I have had feline companions. I do not believe they have suffered any deprivation, and, in fact, have benefited enormously. Many of my pets have lived well in excess of 15 years regardless of breed.

Our modern world is a dangerous place for our beloved animal companions. Whether that danger arises from automobiles, aggressive dogs, wildlife, or bad humans, the risk is not worth it in my opinion. I would never dream of allowing my cats access to the outside world.

There are many cat owners who achieve a compromise position by designing some kind of secure enclosed structure that allows their cats to be contained while enjoying sunlight and fresh air and the sounds of the outside world.

I have done this with my pets, and so long as you can securely bring your cat in and out of the structure, I think this is an excellent idea. There are no set designs for these kinds of enclosures, but you can easily find many good ideas online through your favorite search engine.

Devon Rex Pros and Cons

Assembling a set of "pros" and "cons" associated with any type of animal is not as simple as some people think. These things are very much a matter of personal perception.

I was raised around dogs and am very fond of them, but I have no desire to keep a dog as a pet because I don't want to have to walk one. Other people think the walks are absolutely the best part of dog ownership.

As we move through subsequent chapters, you'll learn more about some of the points I've chosen to list below. I would advise reading the whole text to get an accurate picture of the Devon Rex and of cat ownership in general before you make your decision.

Pros for the Devon Rex

- Highly social, family-oriented cat.
- Good with other pets and children.
- Learns tricks easily.
- Plays fetch and will walk on a leash.
- Active and kittenish for life.
- Unique appearance

Cons for the Devon Rex

- Does not like to be left alone for long periods.
- Talkative, but not raucous like a Siamese.
- Will be in the middle of everything.
- A lap cat, but not aloof.
- Best kept indoors due to the danger of sun exposure.
- Unique appearance.

Chapter 2 – Finding Your Devon Rex

People who have not gone through the process of purchasing a pedigree cat may have some completely erroneous assumptions about what will happen when they visit a cattery.

If you think that you are simply going to drop in, pick a kitten, and pay for it, you need to sit down. It's not going to be that simple, and you may get turned down. Yes. You may get turned down.

If a breeder doesn't think you're a good candidate to raise one of their kittens, they don't have to do business with you — and they won't.

Understanding Breeder Requirements

Expect to be required to sign a written contract that will have some or all of the following stipulations:

- Sometime in the 72 hours following the adoption, you will take the kitten to a qualified veterinarian for a complete health evaluation. You will need to provide proof that this visit has occurred.

- Your agreement that the cat you adopt will be spayed or neutered before it reaches 6 months of age and that you will provide proof of this fact in order to gain possession of the cat's papers.

In addition, you will be asked questions about your home life, your schedule, and your prior experience with cats and with the Devon Rex breed.

If you need to, adjust your attitude now! The breeder is not being a jerk or being nosy. They're doing their job — putting the welfare of the cats they raise first.

You may be asked things like, "Where do you plan for the kitten to sleep?" or "What do you intend to feed your cat?" Be honest with your answers. Don't try to "game" a breeder. It generally backfires.

If this is your first time to have a cat as a pet or to have this breed, say so. Ask questions. For instance, you might say something like, "My last cat loved to sleep on the bed. What do Devon Rex cats usually prefer? I'll get the kitten whatever kind of bed he'd like best".

Breeders want to know that the kitten is going to a good home with loving and attentive "parents." Don't be at all surprised if the breeder calls you up during the first few weeks to check on the progress of the transition. You want this to happen!

Making friends with your breeder gives you access to someone who knows Devon Rex cats well and can answer your questions. This is an important relationship, and one you want to cultivate.

Formulating Your Own Questions

Adopting a pedigree cat should be a process of give and take on both sides in the exchange of information. Any breeder who is not willing to answer your questions should be considered suspect.

In truth, talking to a breeder about their cattery usually opens the floodgates of information. Most are not only willing to talk about their cats, they're impossible to stop!

There are, however, some definite areas that you want to cover pre-adoption. Be sure that you go over these points to your satisfaction.

- Have the kitten's parents been healthy throughout their lives?

- Does the cattery maintain complete health records on all their cats and are you free to examine those records?

- Can you meet and interact with the kitten's parents?

- Has the kitten received any vaccinations and if so, when are the booster shots to be administered?

- Will you receive copies of all of the kitten's records at the time of adoption?

- Are there any specific health problems associated with Devon Rex cats and has the kitten been evaluated for those issues?

- Has the kitten seen a vet for any other reason? If so, why and what treatment was administered?

- What is the nature of the health guarantee that is part of the adoption agreement?

- Has the kitten had fleas and has it required deworming?

- Ask for a complete summary of all veterinary care the kitten has received and copies of the complete records to pass on to your own veterinarian.

Understand that a kitten that has had or even does have fleas is not the end of the world. Catteries fight fleas on an ongoing basis. You just want to make sure that the "passengers" have disembarked from the baby before it comes into your home. Eradicating fleas can be a time consuming and exhausting process once they are established.

Also ask for the breeder's references. These should include people who have adopted kittens from the cattery in the past and who are willing to talk to you about the experience — both in terms of interaction with the breeder and their experience with the cat as a pet.

Ask About Socialization

In most cases catteries keep kittens until they are at least 3 months of age. This ensures that when the babies are adopted they have been fully weaned and they've become trained in the "basics," like litter box and scratching post use.

I'll discuss both of these things in greater detail later in the book, but you do want to specifically ask what kind of box and litter the kitten is accustomed to using and what kind of scratching surface.

The best way to reinforce and encourage good behavior in a newly adopted kitten is to keep everything exactly the same. For a smooth transition, use the same kind of box, litter, and post, only introducing changes gradually as the kitten grows.

Also find out how the breeder works with the kitten to make sure that it is well socialized. Some of the hallmarks of a good program of socialization include:

- Daily handling
- Free exploration time
- Interaction with other cats and kittens

- Intellectual stimulation (toys and games)
- Supervised exposure to dogs and/or children
- Comfort level with reasonable noise

Kittens that have gotten used to these kinds of environmental factors early on tend to show much less nervousness as adult cats and more flexibility and adaptability to changes in their immediate surroundings.

Devon Rex cats have a reputation for being one of the most social of all companion breeds, getting on well with everyone and everything. All cats are individuals, however, and they will react to the manner in which they are raised.

If you've ever seen those funny cartoons that suggest pets and owners look alike, you may understand this point more fully. A nervous person tends to have nervous pets; a grumpy person's pets may be irascible and so on.

Although Devon Rex cats are agreeable, gentle, and friendly, if truly pushed to their limits, they will react. That being said, however, any cat will display ill temper if something is going on that frightens, threatens, or simply displeases it.

Most breeders are in agreement, however, that a well socialized cat of any breed will be much more likely to exhibit the most positive qualities of its kind.

Judging the Health of a Kitten

You are not just visiting a cattery to inspect the facilities and to be evaluated by the breeder, you are also there to look at cats — which is actually the best part!

Always ask permission to handle the cats. Even though it's assumed that you are there to do so, it's just polite. If you're asked to use a hand sanitizer first, don't be offended.

Many feline diseases are so easily transmissible they can be passed from one cat to another with just a nose tap. Sanitizing your hands is for the protection of the cats, and not a reflection on you.

When you are handling the kittens, pay attention to all the following factors:

- The kitten's coat should be soft, clean, and completely intact even though the density may be as fine as suede. There should be no evidence of thin spots or any missing patches of hair. Some Devon Rex kittens do molt, so if you are uncertain about the quality of the coat, discuss the issue with the breeder.

- If the consistency allows, very gently blow on the fur to create a parting. Otherwise, look at the skin as closely as possible. There should be no flaking, which would indicate that the skin is dry.

- Look behind the ears, in the "arm pits," and at the base of the tail. These are the prime locations for evidence of flea "dirt," small accumulations of what looks like tiny gravel, but is actually excreted blood from the fleas.

- Also look inside the ears. The flaps should be pink and healthy in appearance and the ear canal should be clean and free of black, tarry debris. There should be no odor, especially one that smells of yeast.

- Take a good look at the baby's eyes. You should be met with a bright, curious gaze that is both interested and sweet. The eyes should not be "runny" with discharge, and there should be no crusting in the corners.

- Also check the kitten's nostrils for any sign of discharge.

- The baby should not be sneezing or otherwise sniffling.

Don't be surprised if the kitten is a little shy when you're first introduced. That's normal. Within minutes, however, you should be interacting with a little ball of madcap energy!

Expect Paperwork

You are, after all, engaging in a transaction, so anticipate a fair amount of paperwork. The basic agreement will include the following:

- A description of the Devon Rex breed.
- A description of the color and pattern of the specific individual being adopted.
- The gender of the kitten.
- The agreed upon price.
- The names of the parents.
- Contact information for both the buyer and the seller.

Specific provisions of the contract may include:

- A promise to provide ongoing and regular veterinary care including the recommended course of vaccinations.
- Agreement to meet the cat's specific grooming needs on a regular basis.

- A statement that no refund will be provided if that cat is returned for any reason.

Returns are a serious matter for breeders. The paperwork will include your agreement to a provision forbidding the giving away or selling of the cat without the breeder's permission.

Breeders are primarily concerned about the welfare of the cat. They do not want to see the animal wind up in any kind of shelter or pet store. Breeders would rather take kittens back than see that happen.

This is extremely important to emphasize. If at any point you feel that you can no longer keep the cat CONTACT THE BREEDER.

You will have to have the cat tested for ringworm, FELV/FIV, and fecal parasites before you return it, but you will always have a safe place to rehouse your cat if that proves to be necessary.

Required Spaying and Neutering

For the most part, people who work with breeders are acquiring kittens that have been judged to "pet quality". For whatever reason, the animal you are adopting is not considered a proper example of the breed for show or breeding purposes.

Don't let that concern you! You probably won't be able to recognize the flaw even if the breeder tells you what it is!

You will, however, have to agree that before the baby reaches six months of age, it will be spayed or neutered.

Since this is the medically recommended period of time for either surgery to occur, this is a reasonable request by a cattery that has every right to protect its bloodlines.

The typical arrangement is that you do not receive the cat's papers until you have provided the cattery with a veterinary receipt showing that the spaying or neutering procedure has been performed.

Declawing Prohibited

Do not be surprised that the adoption agreement will expressly forbid declawing the cat in strongly worded terms. This surgery is illegal in Europe and in many parts of the United States for the simple reason that it is inhumane and completely unnecessary.

In order to remove the claw, the last digit of the cat's toe must be amputated. The procedure is painful, it affects the animal's mobility for the duration of its life, and it takes away the cat's primary means of self-defense.

Cats that have been introduced to scratching apparatus early in their life and whose claws are regularly clipped are not destructive.

Declawing is a radical measure done exclusively for the convenience of the owner and is a callous disregard of the welfare of the cat.

Known Health Conditions

In the chapter on health, I'll cover some of the medical issues associated with Devon Rex cats, including those that are genetic in nature.

In terms of adoption protocol, just remember that when you are adopting a pedigreed Devon Rex, the paperwork should include a health guarantee.

There should also be a statement about the parents' health, and an indication of what evaluations and tests they have received as well as a statement of the results.

Remember that the requirement for an initial health evaluation on your part, usually within 72 hours of the time you take possession of the kitten, provides a baseline for the health guarantee. This measure protects the cat *and* you.

Preparing to Bring a Kitten Home

If you don't know it already, let me stress something that is pretty much a constant with all cats irrespective of breed — they do NOT like change. From a very early age, most cats get used to things being one way and they'd prefer that not change.

It is especially important when transitioning a kitten from a cattery to your home that everything stays the same, particularly regarding litter box arrangement and food.

Ask the breeder what kind of box the kitten has become accustomed to. You will want to know the style of the box, the height, and the kind of litter used.

Cats are very sensitive about litter texture. An abrupt change can put a cat off its box and lead to all kinds of problems. The same is true of litter box style.

I have had cats that absolutely would not use an open box under any circumstances, demanding the privacy of a covered tray.

Any changes to a cat's routine, especially in regard to the litter box, must be introduced slowly. Go in prepared to meet defeat. There may well be no more stubborn creature on the planet than a cat that has made up its mind about something.

Diet will be discussed at length in the daily care chapter, but you certainly do not want to subject a kitten to an abrupt food change. That is an open invitation for gastrointestinal upset.

Ask the breeder what the kitten has been eating and what dietary program they use with their maturing cats. Follow this advice to the letter, again, only introducing changes very slowly.

You will want to have some kitten safe toys on hand for the baby's homecoming. Don't bother with anything that has catnip. Cats show no reaction to the herb until they are 6 - 9 months old.

Instead, concentrate on items that do not present any kind of choking hazard. Many cat toys will always be "with supervision only" items. These include anything with strings, feathers, bells and similar attached decorations.

Approximate Costs

A pet quality Devon Rex kitten typically sells for $600 - $1000 / £455 - £650 and up. After that, however, the breed is no more expensive to keep than any other popular domestic cat.

For a complete understanding of the monthly costs associated with keeping a cat, please refer to Chapter 3 on daily care.

In the absence of a chronic illness requiring ongoing veterinary care, the bulk of your monthly expenses will be for food and litter. Approximately 75% of the amount will go directly to feeding your pet.

Never Rule Out a Rescue Cat Adoption

Obviously I'm a fan of the Devon Rex breed or I wouldn't be writing this book. I would never discourage anyone from bringing a Devon Rex into their home. But, like a true cat lover, my affections are not limited to pedigreed breeds.

I love all cats, including the Domestic Shorthairs often referred to as "alley cats." My first cat was a black and white tuxedo tom I named Jimmy. He was a Domestic Shorthair that grew into a wonderful, big boy who was a perfect companion for a child.

There's no doubt in my mind that my experience with him colored my perception of all the cats I've known since. I still gravitate toward toms, the bigger the better. So you see, to my mind every individual feline has unique qualities that will endear the cat to someone looking to give the animal a forever home.

This book — indeed any cat book — would be incomplete without praising the work of "no kill" shelters and rescue groups the world over. There are literally hundreds of thousands of lovely cats out there in need of a good home, and I can't say enough about the incredible people who selflessly work on their behalf.

If your heart is set on owning a Devon Rex, you will undoubtedly have a wonderful relationship with your new pet for many years to come. But if you are simply thinking about adopting a cat, and perhaps are already a bit nervous about the cost of a pedigree pet, please don't rule out a rescue adoption.

Giving an abandoned kitten or adult cat a "forever home" is one of the greatest acts of kindness an animal lover can perform, one for which you will be rewarded daily with the affection and loyalty of an animal that might very well have died otherwise.

Check your local shelter and speak with your veterinarian to find rescue groups in your area. I assure you, there will be many. Trap/neuter/release programs work hard every day to stem the raging epidemic of unwanted stray animals, but it is still an epic and tragic problem.

If you do move forward with your plans to adopt a pedigree Devon Rex, please remember the efforts of rescue groups with your kind donations. These endeavors are always underfunded and understaffed. They need your help, but more importantly, the cats need your help!

Human Health Considerations

Before you buy you also need to consider any implications to your own health. For example, do you know if you have an allergy or sensitivity to cats? I would recommend taking advice from your Doctor to ensure that you understand the implications to your own health and if necessary, are allergy tested.

Chapter 3 – Daily Care for Your Cat

The basics of cat care are fairly standard for most breeds, with obvious differences for short and long-haired cats, or even for those, like the Sphinx, that have virtually no hair at all.

A great deal of successful feline husbandry involves understanding life from the perspective of your cat. In the case of the Devon Rex, there's not a lot of guesswork involved. Your highly conversational cat will make his opinions and ideas quite clear, generally from his perch on your shoulder.

Given the active, agile, and highly "bright idea" motivated

personality of your Devon Rex, there are some standard precautions that apply to bringing any kitten into the household that *triple* in importance for this breed. There's a very good reason why most owners are convinced Devons are related to monkeys, and you're about to find out why!

All kittens think they're Bengal tigers and they can get into Bengal tiger-sized trouble fast, but you have no idea what a Devon can conjure up in that inventive mind!

The Need to "Kitten Proof"

Many people underestimate kittens for the simple reason that they are small — or at least you think they are until one gallops over you in the night or goes thundering down the hall.

Take basic steps to "kitten proof" your home like removing potentially toxic houseplants, taping cords and wires to the baseboards, capping electrical outlets, and securing or moving large heavy objects that could get pulled down or knocked over.

The problem with kittens — and this is true of any breed, not just Devon Rex cats— is that they have zero judgment and bottomless delusions of grandeur.

Kitten proofing the house, in this case, is much more about protecting your new little baby than taking care of your stuff. A good place to start is having a look at your houseplants and what you have growing outside.

Beware of Toxic Houseplants

Like many breeds, Devon Rex cats are often tempted to start nibbling on houseplants. Chances are good you won't enjoy the destruction of your plants, but you must also realize that many houseplants are actually quite toxic to cats.

The Cat Fancier's Association has produced a fairly comprehensive list of the most hazardous plants and it is always better to be overly cautious with vegetation and plant life. Of this lot, lilies are especially dangerous.

I appreciate it can be difficult to monitor and physically do anything about neighboring properties but any of the plants on this list should be kept strictly away from cats, and your pet should not be allowed into the garden if you have these items growing there or in your yard.

If your Devon Rex eats any part of a plant you believe to be poisonous, seek the help of a qualified veterinarian immediately.

In Appendix 2, I have itemized this list as I think it is an important resource and I hope you will find it of assistance and reassurance in respect of the plants you may have growing in your garden or yard.

Making an Easy Transition

The best advice on helping your Devon Rex kitten make a smooth transition to life with you will come directly from the breeder. These cats have many things going for them in terms of their adaptability and genial good humor.

Still, you will be bringing home a very young cat. No matter how big a kitten *thinks* he is, he's still a tiny little fellow and coming to live with you means he's leaving everything and everyone he knows. The more you can cushion this transition, the better.

At first, you will want to keep your new pet confined to a relatively contained area, or a completely segregated space if there are other cats in the house.

The best initial introductions with other pets are those conducted via the "sniff test" through a closed bedroom or bathroom door. This generally leads to a little exploratory under-the-door paw play as well.

Face-to-face introductions should always be supervised, but do not intervene unless it's absolutely necessary. Animals will pick up on our emotions. If you are nervous, they will be nervous.

Do not overreact, and if a "rescue" is necessary, just quickly and quietly pick up the kitten and return it to its own "room" until you're ready to try again.

Most cats need about a week to 10 days to become fully acclimatized to new surroundings. That's about the same length of time necessary for the hierarchy to get worked out in multiple pet households.

Don't be surprised if your kitten shoots to the top of that "pecking order". They can be veritable little tyrants, and those tiny claws are very, very sharp.

The Mind of a Cat

It's a commonly held belief that understanding the thought processes of a cat is next to impossible. Your Devon Rex will gaze up at you with those expressive, other-worldly eyes and you'll fall instantly under his spell – all the while knowing that you'll never be able to completely fathom what's going on in that agile feline mind.

In truth, however, the majority of the stereotypes people entertain about cats are completely wrong. While some breeds are more reserved than others, that factor is more an individual trait than a genetic standard. Cats aren't nearly as inscrutable as popular wisdom would have you believe.

It is not uncommon for a cat to single out one person for special affection. While they may be friendly to others in the family, they will lavish their love, loyalty, and attention on their favorite.

Cats are not the self-sufficient loners of the animal world people make them out to be. Some cats will do fine on their own during the day, but they will want your attention at night, even greeting you at the door to hear about your day.

When you bring a pet of any kind into your life, you're not just responsible for its care and feeding in a physical sense. You must also meet your pet's *emotional* needs, which are substantial with a breed as social and intelligent as the Devon Rex.

Most behavior problems stem from an animal that is simply not getting enough attention. Cats get lonely, bored, and unhappy, and they let you know about it in the only ways that are available to them.

We tend to think of things like furniture shredding or knocking things over as a cat being "bad". In reality, those instances are examples of a cat trying to tell you something.

The one situation that absolutely makes me see red, and that I will write about at greater length later in this chapter, occurs when people turn their cats over to shelters due to poor litter box habits.

If you were to go into the home and look at the litter box, in 9 out of 10 cases, it will be filthy. Cats are fastidious creatures with a highly acute and well developed sense of smell. They won't go in a urine-soaked box, and they have definite preferences in regard to litter texture and box design.

Even more serious, however, is the very real possibility that a cat that is going outside of the box has an undiagnosed kidney or bladder condition.

If a cat attempts to urinate in the box and experiences pain, it associates the discomfort with the location. The poor thing is just trying to find a place to go without hurting!

If you are a first-time cat owner, don't fall for such ridiculous and cruel stereotypes. The more you are engaged in your pet's day-to-day life, the better you will understand his language, and the better you can anticipate problems before they occur.

I have owned cats for more than 40 years and can attest to the unique qualities of each as an individual irrespective of breed. The important thing is that you spend time with your pet and learn how he communicates.

Many dog people are quite taken aback to hear that cats know and care when their people have had a bad day, but it's true. Don't be at all surprised to find your Devon Rex expressing genuine and appropriate sympathy and support at just the moment you need it most.

I actually think cats are quite clear in the ways in which they communicate with us; they simply deliver their messages differently than dogs.

Canines are a more effusive species, but cats still get their meaning across quite clearly if you know how to read their body language, facial expressions and vocal intonations.

Dietary and Nutritional Information

Your emphasis in selecting foods for your cat should always be on quality. Based on the advice you initially receive from your breeder, and then from your veterinarian, buy the best food you can afford.

The following information and guidelines will help you to further refine the choices you make to optimize your cat's nutritional intake.

Wet or Dry?

This is the initial question most pet owners' face. The tendency is all too often to go with dry due to the convenience both in serving the food, and in the belief that using dry food will make litter box maintenance easier.

This is a mistake. Cats are carnivores. Wet food provides them with a vital source of hydration, and cats that are fed canned food are less prone to gain weight than those that receive dry food only.

The best choice for your Devon Rex is to feed a healthy mixture of wet and dry food that provides not only the correct mixture of nutrients, but also the tastes and textures your pet will enjoy.

The Devon Rex Appetite

In trying to describe the Devon Rex and his relationship to food, the one word that comes inescapably to mind is "pig." These cats are absolute chowhounds. I have never seen a Devon turn down a meal or fail to beg for food, even if he finished eating five minutes ago.

Don't even think about giving a Devon Rex as much food as he *thinks* he needs. You'll go broke and you'll have a 75 lb. / 34.19 kg cat. Free feeding – the practice of leaving food out all the time – is NOT an option with this breed. Schedule your cat's meals, dole out specific portions, and stick to the program.

Be prepared for the plaintive begging, the woebegone looks, and the delicately raised and imploring paw. There are no lengths to which a Devon will not go to convince you that he is on the brink of starvation. And when that doesn't work? Your lovely cat will resort to rank thievery.

Don't glance away from your plate at the dinner table. Don't leave food out on the counter. Don't let the grocery sacks go unattended for five minutes. In short, do not give a Devon Rex a chance to get at anything edible or it will be gone. They are indiscriminate and omnivorous.

You should be careful with any cat in regard to potentially toxic human foods, but elevate this caution to the tenth power for a Devon Rex.

A Note on Weight

Before we discuss actually choosing foods, let me give you a quick tip on how to judge the shape of your cat's figure.

If you stand over your cat and look down at his body while he is also standing, you should be able to see a slight indentation just behind the rib cage.

This is an excellent sign that your cat's weight is being maintained at a healthy level. If you can't see any "hips," Fluffy is probably getting a little too heavy.

Don't ever let your cats get started on human food. Many of the things we eat simply aren't good for our feline friends (more on that in just a minute), but giving a cat human food is an invitation to health problems.

Once a cat starts to become overweight, it's just a small step to conditions like diabetes, heart problems and joint diseases. Cats are skilled beggars. Use your will power! Don't fall down that slippery slope.

Dangerous "People" Foods

There are many things that we eat every day that a cat should never touch due to their toxicity in the feline system. These items include, but are not limited to:

- alcoholic beverages
- avocados
- grapes / raisins
- eggs
- garlic
- onions
- chives
- yeast dough
- caffeine in any form
- chocolate

The toxic elements present in chocolate are substances called methylxanthines, which are found in cacao seeds. A similar extract is used in soda beverages, which a cat should never be allowed to consume.

Cats that have been exposed to chocolate or to sodas can exhibit symptoms that are severe to the point of being life threatening. These may include:

- excessive thirst
- panting
- vomiting
- diarrhea
- irregular heartbeat
- seizures
- tremors

Sodas also contain sweeteners that include xylitol, which can cause liver failure in cats. Err on the safe side, and keep your pet away from all sweet items.

Salty foods are equally dangerous as they can cause rapid dehydration, creating a serious health risk.

Cats and Milk

Although milk is not necessarily toxic to cats, it's also not the be all and end all of the feline diet as many people believe. A large percentage of cats are as lactose intolerant as their human keepers.

Felines do not produce sufficient amounts of the enzyme lactase. This means they do not efficiently digest cow's milk and are subject to gastrointestinal upset and diarrhea if they are given too much dairy content in their diets.

Adult cats do not require milk and they actually don't get a lot of nutritional value from consuming it. All mammals produce milk that is correct for their own young, and, to state the obvious, cats aren't cows.

You can certainly offer your cat milk or cream occasionally as a treat, but if there is any sign of stomach upset or discomfort, discontinue the practice.

Reading Labels

When you read the label of a food you are considering for your pet, never lose sight of the fact that cats are meat eaters.

If the first item on the label is not meat, look at another food.

As a general rule, the cheaper foods contain much more plant material as filler, while the more expensive or premium foods have a greater amount of meat.

There are so many kinds of cat food on the market it's best to go with breeder and veterinarian recommendations and your own budget in making a specific selection.

Estimating Food Costs

With the great variety of foods on the market, offering a

clear estimate of food costs is all but impossible.

Conservatively, and based entirely on my own experience, you will likely spend $50 / £32.50 each month on wet food with $25 / £16.25 going for dry in the same period.

Given the voracious appetite of the Devon Rex, I suggest limiting the amount of dry food to a quarter to half a cup per day or 2 to 4 ounces / 56.7 to 113 grams. Put out wet food once to twice per day. These servings should be roughly 5.5 ounces / 156 grams each.

Food and Water Bowls

For the most part you will be able to use plain bowls for both food and water, but you do need to be aware of a potential sensitivity called "whisker stress". The problem doesn't show up often in the Devon Rex with their short, curly whiskers, but it's not impossible and may just be a matter of personal taste on the part of the cat.

Some cats just do not like the feeling of their whiskers dragging against the side of a bowl. You can tell that this is happening if your pet routinely picks up food and drops it on the floor to eat it. The whiskers of a Devon Rex are so short and curly they are sometimes compared to a man's beard in the "five o'clock shadow" stage, so whisker stress probably won't be a problem.

If, however, your pet does exhibit this behavior with his food, try switching to a receptacle that is more like a tray to cut down on the irritating sensation for your pet. There are products made specifically for cats for this purpose.

Normal food and water bowls will each cost $5 - $10 / £3.25 - £6.50. Try to use either stainless steel or crockery as plastic has a tendency to cause a breaking out on cat's chins that is commonly referred to as feline acne.

If you do opt for a bowl designed to reduce whisker stress, you will spend about $25 / £16.25. These trays typically come with legs or a stand to make them more stable and are thus slightly more expensive.

Be sure that your cat has a constant supply of clean drinking water. Some cats far prefer to drink running water, and I am a big fan of feline water fountains. These units sell for $30 / £19.50.

The Raw Diet Considered

Many pet owners over the past few years have been attracted to the idea of giving their pets, both dogs and cats, the "raw" diet. The idea is to provide the animals with the kind of nutritional intake they would receive if they were hunting on their own.

Please understand that I mention this here not to advocate the diet or to instruct you in the proper administration of this dietary program. If you are interested in "feeding raw," you must research this topic thoroughly and discuss it with your veterinarian. Be prepared to hear serious reservations.

The majority of veterinarians and many cat experts do not believe that the raw concept is a good one since it includes bones. Even ground, bone shards can severely lacerate a cat's throat and intestines.

This, and the risk of salmonella poisoning, makes raw feeding for cats a questionable proposition. Certainly there is much more to this process than simply putting raw meat in your cat's bowl.

If you are interested in raw feeding, you have to learn how to do it, and you have to have the correct equipment. Strict standards of sanitation must be met, and only raw beef and chicken can be used.

All uneaten food, even if it has been refrigerated, must be discarded after 2-3 days and none of the food can ever be microwaved.

Just because your cat is a carnivore by nature, do not feel that a raw diet is necessary and do not proceed with such a feeding program without expert advice and adequate research.

Managing the Litter Box

In the beginning use the type of box to which the kitten has become accustomed at the breeder's. Also use the same kind of litter.

Any time you decide to try a different box or litter type, always leave the original arrangement in place until you know your cat will use the new option.

If your cat does go outside the box, you must clean the area with special enzymatic cleaners like those produced by Nature's Miracle $5 - $10 / £3.25 - £6.50.

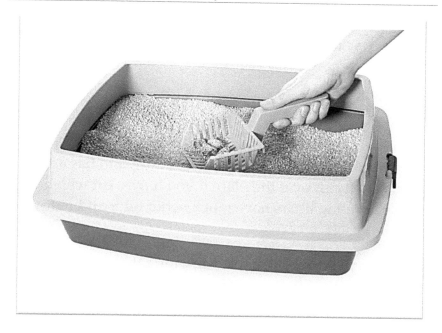

Cats interpret the world as a complex mix of smells. Any time your cat has urinated or defecated on a spot, and can still detect the scents he has left there, he may well consider that place acceptable to do his "business".

Picking a Litter

Whereas once the only commercially available litter was standard clay gravel, there are now many choices for cat owners to consider.

Clay Gravel

Clay gravel remains the tried and true traditional approach and it is also the cheapest. You can purchase 10 lbs. / 4.54 kg of this material for as little as $2.50 - $5.00 / £1.66 - £3.25.

The major drawback with clay gravel is the amount of dust it produces, and its low capacity to absorb moisture and control odor.

Clumping Sand

Clumping sand has become one of the most popular litters on the market. While it also generates dust, and has a capacity to fly all over the place if you have a cat who likes to dig, clumping litters have much better odor and moisture control.

Remember, if you are using a clumping litter, do not flush the clumps unless the mixture specifically says, "flushable". Regular clumping litter will absolutely destroy your plumbing, essentially turning to concrete in your pipes.

Clumping litter is more expensive than clay, but it is available in large amounts, for instance, 42 lbs. / 19.51 kg for $18 / £11.70.

Multiple cat mixes or those that claim extra odor controlling properties may be extremely pricey, however, with only 1.4 lbs. / 0.63 kg retailing for as much as $30 / £19.50.

"Green" Litters

Plant-based cat litters are generally made of materials like pine. They can be cost effective and are certainly environmentally friendly, but not all cats will use them.

Because the shavings are so lightweight, some cats don't seem to think they "feel" right. Never underestimate how sensitive cats are to texture, in many areas of their lives.

If your cat will use green litters, you will pay around $10 / £6.50 for 30 lbs. / 13.61 kg.

Absorbing Crystals

Crystals are the latest innovation in cat litters, and are touted for their ability to cut down on the potential for bacterial growth. The silica gel from which the crystals are made traps urine and holds it, allowing for a dry box and easier clean up.

Again, this is a matter of texture for the cat's paws. Not all cats will use crystals, and they are expensive, albeit effective. On average, 8 lbs. / 3.63 kg of absorbing crystals sells for $16 / £10.40.

Picking a Box

After you have made your choice of litter type, you must consider what kind of box to offer your cat. Again, in the beginning, use what the kitten thinks is "normal" based on its experience at the cattery.

Your major options in this area start with the tried and true open pan. This is a cheap avenue at just $6 - $10 / £3.90 - £6.50, but there are drawbacks.

Open pans allow cats who like to scratch to fling litter far and wide, and they are a nightmare when it comes to dust control.

Many cats don't like open pans because they don't care to be watched. Additionally, open pans are unsightly.

Homeowners have to find some place to both hide the pan and make it accessible to the cat, which can be a challenge.

Covered boxes answer many of these issues, giving the cat privacy, and hiding the mess. Since the lids are typically outfitted with a filter, a covered box will cut down on both dust and odor.

Depending on the size and shape of the box (square, rectangular, round, or triangular to fit in corners), you will spend $30 - $50 / £19.50 - £32.50 for a covered litter box.

The latest innovation is the self-scooping box, which humans love and cats treat with either a certain amount of fascination, suspicion or open horror.

Self-scooping boxes require electricity since they employ a scoop activated by a motion sensor that is tripped when the cat exits the pan. The scoop rakes through the litter, depositing the soiled material in a closed receptacle.

When the receptacle is full, simply cap it with a provided lid and throw it away, putting a fresh disposable refill in its place.

If your cat does not react with fear to the mechanism, this can be an excellent solution for cat owners who are weary of scooping. This kind of automated arrangement costs approximately $150 - $200 / £97.50 - £130.

Be warned. If you decide to try a self-scooping box, keep your old pan in place. Fluffy may well rebel at this idea and demand his old "out house" back.

The Devon Rex at Play

In most breed profiles, you'll see the Devon Rex described with words like agile, energetic, acrobatic or playful. Those adjectives don't even come close to capturing the force of life that is a Devon Rex at play.

They love the more elaborate dangling toys because their human is on the other end of the string, but a Devon will be entertained by anything that presents an intellectual challenge. For this reason, they are receptive to learning tricks, often spontaneously coming up with their own variations on the theme.

Devons excel at the increasingly popular agility course

competitions now held in concert with many cat shows and, thanks to their easygoing, social personalities, they don't mind performing for a crowd. In fact, they seem to love it. If there is one thing I can promise you about life with a Devon Rex it is this; you will have fun.

I can certainly attest to just how much you can spend on cat toys, just remember that some are "supervision only."

Anything that has feathers, string, a squeaker, or a bell should be something your cat has access to only when you're around. These things can be choking hazards, so exercise appropriate caution. But beyond that, the sky is the limit for what a Devon will find entertaining. For this breed, the world is his toy box.

The real trick in picking toys for any breed is to watch and get to know your specific cat and to buy things that cater to his interests and natural inclinations.

Devon Rex cats can be vigorous with their claws, so a scratching post is a must. You can get away with a simple carpeted scratching pole retailing for $30 / £19.50 but you're far better off factoring in the expense of an elaborate cat gym for $100 - $300 / £65 - £195.

With a breed this energetic and acrobatic, get as much of a "jungle" as you can afford -- platforms, tunnels, perches, ramps, hammocks – your Devon Rex will go nuts for it all!

Anything that is outfitted with platforms, tunnels, perches, and ramps will speak to the "jungle beast" in any cat and delight the acrobatic Devon Rex. Frankly, the expenditure on an elaborate "gym" will be just as much for your entertainment as your cat's pleasure.

If your Devon Rex does show an unhealthy interest in your furniture, you can discourage this behavior with pennyroyal or orange essence sprays at $12 - $15 / £7.80 - £9.75 or double-side adhesive strips at $8 - $10 / £5.20 - £6.50.

Speaking Cat

Cats have a complex language that is built not just on vocalizations, but also on facial expression and body language. Most people think, for instance, that when a cat rubs up against his human, it's an expression of affection. Try "ownership".

When your cat is rubbing up against you, he's using the scent glands located around his mouth to mark you as his territory. Now, granted, you may have "most favored nation" status, but the rubbing has pretty much the same purpose whether it's you or the edge of the coffee table.

When a cat leans into you with his whole weight or "bonks" you with his head, this is more of an expression of camaraderie and affection - and likely a request for an ear scratching or a chin rub. This is the same message a cat is sending when he positions himself between you and the laptop screen or plops down on your book.

When a cat picks up his paw and shakes it with an expression of disgust, he's clearly saying, "I don't like how this feels, smells or tastes. Yuck!"

A cat that has just broken a flower pot won't apologize, but he's smart enough to know you're not going to be thrilled with him, so being elsewhere is, in his mind, a great idea.

While many of these cues are universal to all cats, remember that every cat is an individual. The real way to "get" your cat's message is just cultivating familiarity over long association. Most cat owners don't need interpreters to know what their cat is saying or to figure out the opinion their pet is expressing.

All dyed in the wool cat people know, "the look," which is usually delivered with withering proficiency right after you've put something sub-standard in kitty's bowl. "The look" is a commentary on human intelligence, and we don't rate well in that moment!

Grooming Requirements

The Devon Rex is fantastically low maintenance. Because their hair is somewhat fragile, brushing is not recommended.

Typically a wipe down with a warm washcloth and gentle drying is more than enough, with the occasional quick shampoo if it's truly required. Devons are quite compliant with this chore when it is required.

Always use a hypoallergenic shampoo especially formulated for use with cats. These products sell in a price range of $10 - $15 / £6.50 - £9.75 for 16 ounces / 454 grams.

If a bath is necessary, do not let your pet's ears get wet and keep all water and shampoo out of the eyes. Working in a sink or tub, lightly shampoo the cat, and rinse the coat completely clean by pouring lukewarm water in a controlled stream over the back.

Gently towel dry the cat moving in the direction of the fur. Do not scrub or rub at the coat. Wrap the Devon in a clean towel and keep your pet warm until its coat is thoroughly dry.

Claw Clipping

With their usual equanimity, Devons are quite good about the matter of having their claws clipped. Claw clipping generally can be done safely at home, and is always the first step in a professional grooming session. To complete this chore safely:

- Place your Devon Rex on your lap.

- Pick up one front paw.

- Apply gentle pressure with your thumb behind the toes.

- With the claws extended, examine the nail.

- The claw is translucent.

- The vascular "quick" is pink.

- Snip off only the clear tips.

- Do not forget the dewclaw on the side of the foot.

Be extremely careful not to nip the "quick" as this will not only cause your pet pain, but result in profuse bleeding. This area is the hardest to reach on most cats, but just go slow and be gentle; your Devon will be patient with you.

Try not to hold your cat down. "Less restraint" is better because no cat likes to feel trapped. With practice, you can safely and quickly trim your pet's nails before the cat even realizes what is happening.

Buy clippers specifically designed for pets. Those with plier grips are easy to use and offer superior control. They are priced at approximately $10 / £6.50.

If you are in any way nervous about doing this, it would be a wise precaution to ask your vet to show you how to trim your cats nails on the first occasion so that you have complete confidence when doing it.

Caring for the Ears

Beyond a gentle wiping down of the earflap with a warm cloth or a cotton ball dipped in warm water, any advanced ear care or cleaning should be left to your veterinarian. Do not ever insert a cotton swab in the ear canal.

Excessive thick, tarry debris and a yeasty smell indicates the presence of ear mites, necessitating a visit to the veterinarian.

Evaluating Professional Groomers

The temptation may be to think that the Devon Rex, like many pedigreed cats, would benefit from the occasional professional grooming, but this is not a hard and fast requirement of ownership and care. As I have already mentioned, due to the nature of its coat, special care should be taken to ensure no damage occurs through unrequired brushing or washing. However, if you need assistance with other aspects of it grooming such as claws, you may prefer to have a professional groomer take care of this.

Under the best circumstances, you will be able to find a groomer who will come to your home. Very few cats of any breed like to be taken out of their familiar environment. Cats are always calmer when everything around them is "theirs."

Ask your breeder for references for local groomers, and inquire at your vet clinic. Most practices keep a bulletin board in the waiting room where groomers and pet sitters leave their flyers or business cards.

Always visit a grooming facility or interview a groomer before booking an appointment for your pet. You want to see how the animals are secured against escape and ensure that the place is clean and well maintained.

Specifically ensure that the establishment requires all client animals to be current with their vaccinations. Feline diseases are highly contagious, so the cats should be kept strictly separated while on the premises.

Grooming costs can vary rather widely, but typically a single session will cost approximately $50 / £32.50

Time Away from Your Cat

All pet owners face one common concern: What happens when it is time to go on vacation? Many people travel with their pets, but the fact is pets cannot always go with their families. What will you do with your cat when you have to go away from home – on vacation or out of town for business or for a funeral, for example?

Consider who will look after your cat before the need ever arises. You have several options. Perhaps a friend or a family member, who has been around your cat and feels comfortable, can call to your home to care for it.

Pet sitters are also a popular option, especially in the United States where pet sitting businesses must be licensed and insured to operate. A pet sitter generally comes to your home to visit your pet – to ensure he has food, water, and time out to exercise. Pet sitters typically charge per visit, and you can schedule several visits each day.

Is a pet sitter a viable option for your cat? That depends. How long will you be gone? Can you afford to have the pet sitter come each day to ensure your cat is looked after as you wish? Be sure, if you look for a pet sitter, to find someone who has experience caring for cats. Before you hire a pet sitter or agree to a visiting schedule, the pet sitter will generally come to your home for an initial consultation. During that meeting, you will talk with the pet sitter about your cat, its schedule, diet, and any other concern you may have. But, more importantly, the meeting will allow your cat and the pet sitter to meet and to become comfortable around each other. Some pet sitters charge for this initial meeting, but many do not.

You can find pet sitters in the United States through the National Association of Pet Sitters (www.petsitters.org) and Pet Sitters International (www.petsit.com). A comprehensive list of pet sitters in the United Kingdom can be found through the National Association of Registered Pet Sitters (www.dogsit.com) and yes, they look after more than dogs and don't have any trouble with cats!

Make sure that your pet sitter is insured and fully referenced as they will have access to you home and your pet. You should also contact your home insurance providers to confirm your cover is not affected by having a pet sitter stay at your home.

If you do not like the idea of a pet sitter, then some rescue organizations offer boarding and pet sitting services while others may just be able to provide you with recommendations of sitters.

If you have trouble finding someone you trust or don't want to become a burden to family and friends then you may want to consider boarding.

Boarding Your Devon Rex

If it should prove necessary to board your Devon Rex while you are away or due to other life circumstances, you'll find that your pet will tend to react to the experience with his usual calm demeanor.

In all likelihood, you will be much more nervous than your cat! If your regular veterinarian does not offer boarding services, here are some guidelines to help you choose a boarding facility:

- Begin checking out facilities well in advance of your trip, especially if it coincides with a major holiday. These places fill up quickly.

- If possible, find a boarder that caters to cats only or that keep their feline clients well segregated from dogs and other pets. Especially when they are in an unfamiliar area cats like quiet.

- Make sure that your pet's food and water intake is closely monitored, especially in the first 24-48 hours. Cats can become dehydrated quickly when they are stressed, which can lead to serious health problems.

- If there is a health problem, does the facility have a vet on staff and what provisions can be made for that person to immediately contact your cat's regular vet?

- Will your cat require any vaccinations or boosters before being allowed to board at the establishment? Do you need to supply any medical records prior to the stay?

- Make sure that your cat will be housed in a spacious enclosure alone. Cats, unlike dogs, do not want to mingle. Additionally, many feline diseases are highly communicable by nothing more than a nose tap.

- If you have more than one cat and will be boarding both, make sure they will be allowed to remain together in the same enclosure.

Be sure to schedule a time to tour the facility. Ask for references, and discuss the facility you are considering with your veterinarian.

Always transport your cat in a secure cat carrier. Never allow your pet to ride in the car unless it is inside its crate, which should be securely locked.

Coming Home Again

How will your cat react when you return home, especially if you have been gone a considerable period? Well, cats are like people, so do not be surprised if your beloved friend is angry with you for having left them. And, like people, he will need time to shed that anger. On the other hand, cats while being extremely independent may just give you a look that says "Oh it's you!" and then won't leave your side for days in case you disappear again.

Chapter 4 – Senior Moments

Not all cats age the same way, any more than all humans experience the same age-related problems. I have had cats with arthritis, one that went blind, and others that developed benign fatty tumors called lipomas.

The signs of aging tend to be gradual. Some of the most typical are included in this chapter.

Less Acute Senses

You may begin to notice subtle signs that your cat is not hearing or seeing as well as it once did. These changes may, however, completely escape your attention.

Some years ago one of my senior cats who went blind compensated so well that I had no idea anything was wrong until I rearranged the living room furniture.

Her obvious confusion led me to schedule a vet visit and we discovered that not only was she blind, but that she was suffering from high blood pressure and needed medication. It might just as easily have been cataracts that were causing the problem.

Obviously no cat that has vision or hearing loss should ever be allowed outdoors. I am not a fan of "outside" cats anyway, as our modern world is far too dangerous for our beloved pets.

Frankly, I would be more concerned about your cat's senses of smell and taste. Deficits with these two abilities can adversely affect your pet's appetite and lead to weight loss. Cats won't eat what they can't smell, so it may be necessary to alter an older cat's diet.

Consult with your vet first so that you don't give a senior cat something that will cause gastrointestinal upset. If your cat isn't used to eating "fishy" foods, they may like the smell, but get an upset tummy from the richer fare.

You can try just slightly warming your pet's existing wet food to increase the smell, but be very careful not to get it too hot. If you warm the food in the microwave, stir it well with a fork and let it cool to just slightly more than room temperature before you give it to your cat. Please ensure that any uneaten food is thrown away quickly to avoid the risk of bacterial growth and the food spoiling.

Changes in Appearance

It's perfectly normal for cats to lose muscle mass as they age, but always have any dramatic changes in weight, both losses and gains evaluated by your veterinarian.

Also pay close attention to the condition of an aging cat's coat. If your pet is not able to groom as well as he once did, you may need to step in and help with more frequent brushing.

Since the Devon Rex coat is somewhat fragile, be especially mindful about any thinning or matting. Both are signs of potential bad health.

Cats can develop arthritis the same way humans do and your pet may simply not be able to reach the hard spots any more. This may extend to "personal" areas.

Without annoying your cat, just make sure all is well around the anal area. If cleaning there is necessary, gently use a warm washcloth and plain, clean water. Please ensure that you observe good hand hygiene and wash the cloth between uses.

Make sure the litter box is low enough for your pet to get in and out of easily. Since cats don't like changes in box type or litter consistency, consider trimming down the front edge of the box so your pet can step in and out more easily.

Changes in Mood and Behavior

The most important thing to do with a senior citizen cat is to be aware of subtle changes in mood and behavior. An older cat may no longer be able to jump up to the window sill, but would still like to sun. Give him a way to "stair step" to his favorite perch without jumping.

Devon Rex cats have a high level of natural activity. While it is true that older cats spend more time sleeping, that fact may just bring a Devon to a level that would be considered "normal" for other breeds. If your Devon does really slow down noticeably, an evaluation by the vet is a good precaution.

Always remember that cats instinctively hide their pain and illness. Use your judgment and your understanding of your pet's nature. Never hesitate to schedule a vet visit. I always give the same advice, "If you think something is wrong with your cat, it probably is".

The last thing you need to worry about is being labeled a "crazy cat lady" or a "doting Dad". You know your pet better than anyone. Go with your gut, especially when it comes to older cats. Make the vet appointment if you think your cat is sick or just not doing well.

Regular Checkups

Make sure your older cat has regular checkups. Seniors are more likely to develop dental issues, and all skin growths should be evaluated.

Monitor changes in litter box habits that might signal a urinary tract infection or more serious kidney problems. If the cat is vomiting more than usual, a vet visit may be in order.

Drinking large amounts of water might indicate the presence of diabetes Aging cats can also suffer from hyperthyroidism and high blood pressure, both of which are very treatable.

Because older cats sleep more, they are more prone to be cold. Make sure your senior has a warm bed and lots of quiet time. The warmth will also help if your pet is suffering from arthritis.

Treat your aging cats like what they are, little ladies and old gents with fur. Love them all the same, and make whatever changes you need to in their environment to keep them happy, engaged, and comfortable in their golden years.

Making the Hard Decision

Saying good-bye to a beloved companion of many years is both heartbreaking and a great act of love. Euthanasia is a difficult topic, both for you to read about and for me to write about.

I can only share with you what I believe to be the truth based on my personal experience. No one can tell you when it is time to make the hard decision but your cat.

Do not listen to anyone who makes you feel pressured to come to a decision. I promise you that you would resent this in the future if you do so.

Get the best medical information that you can from your veterinarian, conduct your own research, and simply be with your cat. I cared for a well-loved pet through a 25-month struggle with cancer.

The people in my life knew better than to try to offer advice. My veterinarian was kind, professional and honest. I will admit I spent money on treatments and medications I could not afford for the simple reason that my pet was enjoying his life and was still very much himself.

The day that he was not, he told me so. Only an "animal person" may understand what I mean, but I assure you my cat told me it was time to go. When he did, I called the vet and we gently and lovingly, helped him through that transition.

I have observed euthanasia from the perspective of a breaking heart. I can tell you with great certainty that when performed by caring, understanding veterinary professionals this is the ultimate act of compassion. My vet had a relationship both with my pet and with me. She remains my good friend and I will always be grateful to her for the care she gave my feline companion to the very last moment of his life.

I cannot stress enough how important it is for you as a pet owner to have a vet with whom you can work in this way. I know this experience would have been truly horrible had I been dealing with a vet who did not understand both my cat's illness and my own emotional pain.

In the aftermath, allow yourself to grieve. You may have to find other "animal people" who will truly understand the loss you are suffering, but be assured that it is a valid loss of a living creature that has been part of your life and a member of your family.

The kindest thing anyone said to me as I struggled to keep my composure in the days following my pet's death was simply, "I am so sorry you lost your friend".

Our pets give us unconditional love, even when we are not being our best selves. The absence of that constancy is a deep loss and one that neither you nor anyone in your life should attempt to minimize.

Adopting a Senior Cat

People who adopt grown cats in need, especially seniors are, in my estimation very special angels. Many lovely older pets are put down every year when all they need is a loving second home.

You will be taking in an animal with established habits and preferences, and likely pre-existing needs, but there is no reason to think you cannot have a loving relationship with an older animal in its golden years.

If you are prepared to meet the special needs of a senior cat, including late in life veterinary expenses, giving an older, homeless cat a home is a vital part of feline rescue work. This is an area of that mission that always needs more willing volunteers.

Chapter 5 – Devon Rex Cat Health

Ongoing preventive health care is the greatest medical service you can provide for your Devon Rex. Think of yourself as your cat's primary health "insurance." The longer you live with your cat, the more you will know what is "normal" for your Devon Rex.

One of the best pieces of advice cat owners can take to heart is this: if you think something is wrong with your pet, then something probably is. Never hesitate to take a companion animal to the vet for fear of being perceived as an over-protective "parent".

Cats hide sickness and pain for as long as they possibly can. This behavior is part of their survival instinct. As small carnivores, they have an innate awareness of their place in the food chain.

In the wild, the appearance of weakness increases the chance of potential predation from larger animals. Even the safest house cat cannot overcome the power of that instinct.

Finding a Vet

Sometimes the best way to find a great local vet is to ask others who own cats. If you do not know someone in your neighborhood with a cat, contact your local animal rescue or go online and find an online discussion group in your area and start asking for recommendations.

In addition to helping you find a good, qualified vet, other cat owners can help you avoid the not-so-desirable vets. Ask plenty of questions as to why the person recommends the particular vet. Is the vet personable and knowledgeable about cats in general? Does he or she have experience? Are his or her prices reasonable, in the person's opinion? Find out as much as you can as to why the person likes the vet. Also ask them what they do not like about the vet.

The Basics of Preventive Health Care

While interacting with your cat on a daily basis, be aware of all the following signs of potential illness and follow up with a vet should any of the symptoms or behavioral changes appear in your Devon Rex.

Changes in weight.

This can mean either a gain or a loss. Cats with a healthy weight have a pad of fat over the ribs, but the bones can still be felt through this layer. Looking down at the cat, you should be able to see an indentation behind the rib cage where the "hips" start.

Physical changes in gait including a reluctance to perform certain motions like running or jumping.

Essentially when a cat displays these kinds of "favoring" behaviors, there is a strong chance the animal is experiencing joint or muscle pain, or that a growth is inhibiting normal movement.

Differences in the level of moisture on the nose.

This can extend to either a dry nose or an actual runny nose indicating the presence of a cold or an infection. A cat's nose under normal circumstances should be clean and dry, but not cracked. There should be no discharge from the nostrils, either clear or discolored.

Presence of discharge from the eyes.

All cats occasionally get an accumulation of "matter" in the eyes, but you should consult your vet if it is excessive and/or persistent. Always make sure the pupils of the eyes are equal and centered and that the whites are not discolored and have only minimal visible blood vessels.

Ear sensitivity and visible debris.

All cats have a tendency to develop ear infections and to

occasionally have problems with ear mites and similar irritating parasites. A foul odor emanating from the ear is always a key warning sign.

The inner surface of the ear should be clean and smooth in appearance with no visible redness. If the area is inflamed, hot to the touch, and/or black debris is present, the cat's ears should be examined by the vet.

Pale gums and yellow discoloration on the teeth.

A cat's gums should be pink, and the teeth should be clean and white. Any dark or yellow build-up on the teeth is an indication that plaque is present.

Regular dental exams are also critical in detecting any lesions that might indicate the presence of an oral cancer. If found early, such growths can be managed with some success.

Dental care is an extremely important aspect of feline husbandry, with many cat owners actually brushing their cat's teeth using feline toothpaste and brushes available at the veterinary clinic. Never use human products for this purpose on a cat.

While such a regimen may sound absolutely impossible, if started early in a cat's life, the animals are often quite amiable about the whole business. Since it's much more a matter of just getting the paste in the cat's mouth, some owners use their index finger as a "brush".

A dental care kit from a vet typically costs about $7 - $10 / £4.55 - £6.50. It's never too late to start looking after your cat's teeth, and it's certainly worth a try to see how your cat will respond to the process.

Don't worry. You won't lose a finger. If your cat doesn't want any part of dental care, he'll let you know fast enough!

What else to look out for.

There are other factors to consider in monitoring your cat's health on a daily basis.

- Have any growths, masses, or bumps evaluated.

- Watch your cat's respiration. It should be from the chest, not the abdomen.

- If the cat goes outside the litter box, immediately have your pet evaluated for kidney and/or bladder infections.

Routine Elements of Health Care

No element of routine health care for your cat is more important than forging a positive relationship with a qualified veterinarian.

While it is true that any "small animal" vet can treat your Devon Rex, I am an advocate of feline-specific practices when they are available.

Offices that are "cats only" tend to be much quieter and have fewer disturbing and threatening scents, which is soothing for patients with a nervous disposition.

The Devon Rex is typically not a nervous cat. They travel well, and don't mind being in the car, but no pet likes to go to the doctor — any more than we do! In my opinion, the calmer the environment at the vet clinic, the better the visit will be for you and your pet.

Any time you are considering using a veterinarian, it's a good idea to make an appointment just to interview the doctor. Explain why you are coming in and that you are perfectly willing to pay the usual fee.

Prepare any questions you have in advance. Be on time. Get the information you need, ask for a brief tour of the clinic, and do not overstay your welcome. Vets are busy medical professionals.

You want to get a sense of the vet's personality and the demeanor of the staff as well as the environment and condition of the clinic itself. Only if you are satisfied with what you see and hear should you make a second appointment to take your cat in.

Even at this point in time, however, don't consider the relationship a "done deal". Observe how the vet and the staff interact with your cat, and how your pet reacts to them. This is not just a matter of you getting along with the vet, but of your cat being as comfortable as possible under the circumstances.

Spaying and Neutering

When you adopt a pet quality Devon Rex from a breeder you will be required to agree to have your pet spayed or neutered before six months of age.

If you do not already have a veterinarian, this will be your first opportunity to get your pet established with a health care professional, so you will want to make careful decision in regard to these procedures.

Prices for spaying and neutering vary by clinic, and there are low cost options available for as little as $50 / £32.50, but this may not be the time to think about economy. Take the time to find a vet with whom you plan to work over the course of your cat's life.

It is a tremendous benefit to your cat's long-term well-being for all of its records to be in one place, and for one health care professional to have followed the cat's development through life. If you need a recommendation for a qualified vet, ask your breeder.

Vaccinations

Vaccinations have long been considered a standard aspect of preventive care for small companion animals, but the practice of administering these injections has not been without controversy in recent years. The primary concern is for the potential of tumors developing at the site of the injection.

If you have concerns about the wisdom of vaccinating your Devon Rex you should discuss this matter with both the breeder and your veterinarian.

By the time you take possession of the kitten, it will undoubtedly have received the first round of shots, so you will have to decide if you wish to finish the course of injections or not.

The recommended course of inoculations includes the following vaccines:

Distemper Combo

This injection is administered at six weeks of age with recommended boosters every 3-4 weeks until the cat is 16 weeks old. A second booster will then be given at one year, with subsequent shots every three years for the remainder of your pet's life.

The standard injection is formulated to provide protection for panleukopenia (FPV or feline infectious enteritis), rhinotracheitis (FVR, an upper respiratory / pulmonary infection), and calicivirus (which causes respiratory infections).

There are variations of the vaccine that also provide protection against Chlamydophilia, which causes conjunctivitis.

Feline Leukemia

At 2 months of age the injection for feline leukemia is administered, with a booster to be given 3 - 4 weeks later. At one year of age, boosters are then given annually for life.

Feline leukemia is an extremely infectious disease that requires only a nose tap for transmission to occur between animals. If your pet is at any risk of coming into contact with cats that live outdoors, this vaccination is extremely important.

Rabies

Often owners do not have a choice about the administration of the rabies vaccine as it is mandated by local law. Proof of compliance is often required as well. Rabies vaccinations are priced at approximately $40 / £26.

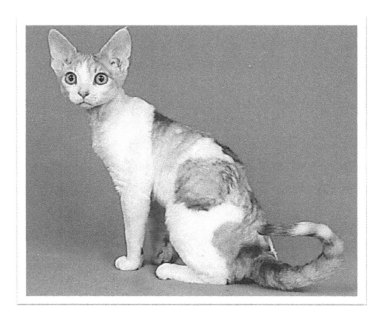

Genetic Conditions

Certainly, overall health should be among the topics you discuss with your breeder while negotiating an adoption. Devon Rex cats are generally vigorous and healthy. They were, however, consciously cultivated from a mutation, so there are potential genetic issues.

Congenital Hypotrichosis

As I discussed previously, a Devon's coat can change throughout the cat's life. Some individuals have fur so short it has the look and feel of suede. If, however, a specific autosomal recessive gene is present, kittens may be born with congenital hypotrichosis. They will have only a very fine, downy coat that will fall out during the first few weeks of life. Other abnormalities may include lack of whiskers, claws, and tongue papillae.

There is no one treatment for the condition. Care usually focuses on improving skin quality with highly emollient shampoos and creams rich in fatty acids. When the cat reaches puberty or shortly thereafter, a fine coat will begin to grow in.

Devon Rex Myopathy

Devon Rex Myopathy, often referred to as "spasticity," can occur in Devon Rex kittens of either gender from 3 weeks to 6 months of age. The severity of the condition, which is an autosomal recessive trait, varies. The disease can be either static or progressive.

Symptoms include:

- Overall muscle weakness, with localized severity in the muscles of the head and neck. The shoulder blades exhibit dorsal protrusion that worsens over time.

- The cat will walk with a high-stepping gait that is most prevalent in the forelimbs and is accompanied by head bobbing. The stride will become progressively shorter with evident muscle tremors and ultimate collapse.

- Affected kittens tire easily and tend to rest with their forepaws on any nearby object that is raised, adopting a position much like that of a dog begging.

- A complication called "megaesophagus" may also be present. It is an enlargement of the esophagus with an accompanying failure of peristalsis that inhibits normal swallowing. This causes regurgitation, and can lead to aspiration pneumonia.

- Because the kitten cannot hold its head properly, there are frequent instances of laryngospasm typically after eating. These episodes can be fatal.

Excitement, stress, concurrent illness, or cold temperatures can exacerbate any of these symptoms.

There is no treatment for Devon Rex Myopathy. Kittens show deterioration for 6-9 months at which time the disease either stabilizes or slows in progression. The ultimate prognosis depends on how much the pharynx is affected

Hemophilia

Devon Rex breeders have worked hard to prevent instances of inbreeding that can lead to hemophilia in cats with Type B blood. It is important, however, to know your cat's blood type so that should surgery ever be required, proper precautions can be taken.

Malassezia Pachydermatitis

Malassezia pachydermatitis is yeast found most often on the skin and ears. If the yeast overgrows it can cause ear infections, seborrhea, erythema and pruritis.

Seborrhea is the excessive discharge of sebum or oil from the sebaceous glands. Erythema is superficial reddening of the skin, and pruritis is severe itching. Hair loss, scaled skin, and foul smelling discharge are also possible.

Treatment includes topical fungicides and medicated shampoos. If there are concurrent bacterial infections antibiotics will also be necessary.

Mismatched Blood Types

Mismatched blood types are a danger in breeding the Devon Rex. When this occurs, kittens in a litter have a different and incompatible blood type from the mother, and are not protected from the antibodies in the milk when nursing.

To avoid this fatally potential condition, breeders must have their cats blood tested before breeding so they can be paired with a sire or dam of the same blood type.

If, however, this problem does occur, the kittens can be fed by hand and allowed to bond with the mother so long as her nipples are covered. You should never contemplate breeding your Devon Rex without the advice and guidance of an expert breeder and a knowledgeable veterinarian.

Other Health Issues

The following are a list of conditions that all cats can develop. The Devon Rex is no more susceptible than any other breed, and while not wanting to give an encyclopedic approach in respect of health or to be anyway alarmist, I've listed several conditions I feel you should be aware of. With the possible exception of periodontal disease, the other issues are fairly rare.

Feline Mucopolysaccharidosis

Certain bloodlines have a higher risk of carrying the Feline Mucopolysaccharidosis IV gene. This condition is caused by a deficiency of arylsulfatase B, primarily in the tissues of the eye which can lead to vision problems.

The same deficiency may also contribute to joint problems and paralysis. The treatment options for this disease include enzyme replacement therapy and bone marrow transplant.

Hairballs

Typically, if a cat is not brushed or combed regularly, the animal ends up swallowing a significant amount of hair while grooming. The resulting hairballs can lead to blockages in the intestines, which may contribute to a number of serious problems.

In these instances, the cat will typically stop eating. A veterinary visit including an X-ray will reveal the offending hairball, and in extreme cases surgery may be required to clear the mass.

Given the texture and quality of the Devon Rex coat, hairballs are rarely an issue with this breed. They shed very little, and their hair is so fine that brushing and combing are not recommended. Do not be alarmed, however, if your cat coughs small hairballs, which is perfectly normal for any feline.

Hip Dysplasia

A defect in the hip socket causes the condition known as hip dysplasia. A cat affected by this problem will move slowly and show a marked reluctance to jump or climb.

The condition presents with a range of severities from mild and annoying to painful and debilitating. Again, there is no way to guarantee that the defect will not show up in any breed of cat.

Maintaining a normal, healthy body weight is a critical component of managing hip dysplasia over a cat's lifetime.

Medication may be required for pain control, and at times corrective surgery is indicated.

Periodontal Disease

Periodontal disease or gum disease is a fairly common problem and involves the inflammation of the supporting structures and tissues around a tooth.

Food particles that get stuck in the cat's gum line will eventually form plaque, which when mixed with minerals and saliva, forms calculus. This substance causes inflammation in the gums called gingivitis.

The most common sign of gingivitis is reddening of the gums. Without treatment, the calculus can build up under the cat's gums and eventually separate the teeth. Bacteria will begin to grow in these spaces, resulting in irreversible periodontal disease.

Other conditions resulting from this occurrence may include bone loss, tissue damage and pus formation. The best treatment for periodontal disease is to control plaque during the early stages with regular tooth brushing and dental checkups.

Polycystic Kidney Disease (PKD)

Polycystic Kidney Disease (PKD) presents at birth with cysts in the kidneys. As the cat ages, the masses grow until they cause the kidneys to fail. PKD becomes detectable in the first 10 years of life; sometimes by the time the animal is 3 years old.

Potential symptoms can include poor appetite and weight loss, extreme thirst and excessive urination, and deterioration of the coat. The cat's gums will be pale from dehydration and it will have bad breath and often ulcers in the mouth. X-rays will show enlargement of the kidneys.

With special diets, the regular administration of subcutaneous fluids, hormone therapy, and antacids, PKD can be managed, but it cannot be cured. The prognosis varies by individual from months to years.

Administering Medications

If you have already had cats in your life, you may have started chuckling just reading the header "administering medications".

Like any sub-culture, "cat people" have their own language. If told by another cat person, "I had to give my cat medicine," the response will likely be the rueful question, "The pink stuff?"

That's a reference to a typical antibiotic given to cats for a number of health problems. It is bright pink and administered with an eyedropper. To say that most cats do not like the "pink stuff," is something of a misnomer.

What cats don't like is being physically restrained while their mouths are pried open and an unwanted liquid is squirted down their throats. Think about that for a minute and you might realize you wouldn't like it either.

There have been great advances in methods of delivery for veterinary medications. When I had a cat suffering from high blood pressure, her medication was a topical cream applied to the inside of the earflap for absorption.

Some medications come as powders that can be hidden effectively in wet food, or even as flavored chews that are sufficiently tasty to cats to be seen as "treats". It isn't always a matter now of holding down an angry, squirming cat and trying to get your pet to swallow liquid or a pill.

When pills and liquids are necessary, I won't lie to you. It can be "game on," with the cat holding a distinct advantage. Never underestimate the level of a cat's determination *not* to do something.

Don't think for a minute that you can hide a pill in a cat's food! Your pet will eat the food and you'll find the pill in pristine condition in the bottom of the bowl.

If you have to give your cat a pill, I recommend a direct, sure and fast approach. Gently take hold of the cat's head from above. Use the index finger of your free hand to open the cat's mouth.

Put the pill as far back in the throat as you can. Gently hold the cat's mouth closed and try stroking your pet's throat to encourage swallowing. Vets have devices called pill "guns" that help to position the pill in the back of the mouth, but I've never been very good with them.

My theory is that the less fuss you make about it all, and the less chance you give the cat to run the show, the more successful you will be. Many people recommend wrapping your pet in a towel first, but I think that just sends the message, "We're getting ready to do something you won't like".

I have found that the same method works well with liquid medication, but I do not like to use the droppers that come with these preparations. I ask for an empty syringe with a mark to indicate dosage.

With the syringe, you benefit from a little more forceful "squirting" of the liquid that further encourages the cat to swallow. If the medicine in question is indeed the "pink stuff," expect your cat to have a little pink fur for a few days (and if I were you, I wouldn't wear white while dispensing the meds).

For any other kind of medications that might have to be administered in the home setting, rely on your vet's advice and ask for a demonstration. I have even given my pets subcutaneous fluid IVs at home. With proper instruction, any home treatment is possible.

Chapter 6 – Pet Insurance and Planning Ahead

Pet insurance is a relatively new option and one about which owners have many questions. Advances in health care procedures for companion animals have substantially improved the lives of our beloved cats and dogs and extended their life expectancy in fantastic ways, but few if any of these procedures are inexpensive.

Is pet insurance worth the expense? Just as is the case with health insurance for humans, you must understand the reasoning behind paying for a policy. Insurance is intended to help address unexpected large expenses that would represent a serious financial strain if paid out of pocket.

In survey results, significant numbers of pet owners admit they would spend any amount of money to save their pet's life. I have, on more than one occasion, gone into debt to pay for medical treatment for one of my cats.

Thankfully, I have not been put in a position to make an end-of-life decision for one of my pets based on financial hardship, but countless pet owners are put in this horrible position every day.

As companies offering health insurance have grown in number and sophistication, it is now possible to customize policies to select deductible level and copay options (termed "agreed excess levels" in the UK) to arrive at premiums that both protect your pet and fit into your budget.

Having an insurance policy will also broaden your options for treatment should your pet require the services of a specialist. In my case, one of my pets needed radiation treatment for an oral cancer. I borrowed the money, and spent the next four years paying his bills.

Do understand, however, that pet insurance reimbursement works a little differently than the regularly accepted human model:

- You pay the vet directly.

- You are responsible for filing the claim.

- You receive the reimbursement directly.

The reimbursement will include eligible expenses minus the level of your deductible and copy according to the set limits of the policy.

A comprehensive insurance policy for a cat including coverage for accidents, illnesses, and some hereditary conditions with an option for chronic condition coverage can be purchased for $15 - $25 / £9.75 - £16.25 per month depending on the deductible chosen.

Typically such policy caries up to $14,000 / £9,100 a year in benefits and is renewable on an annual basis.

Ask plenty of questions to determine the best company and plan for your needs:

- Can you go to your regular vet, or do you have to go to a vet assigned by the pet insurance company?

- What does the insurance plan cover? Does it cover annual exams? Surgeries? Emergency illness and injury?

- Does coverage begin immediately?

- Are pre–existing conditions covered? In addition, if your cat develops a health issue and you later have to renew the policy, is that condition covered when you renew your policy?

- Is medication covered?

- Do you have to have pre–authorization before your pet receives treatment? What happens if

your cat has the treatment without pre–
authorization?

- Does the insurance policy cover dental issues
and chronic health problems?

- Is there a lifetime maximum benefit amount?
If so, how much is that amount? A benefit
plan with a lifetime maximum of only a few
hundred dollars surely will not suffice!

- Is there an amount that you have to pay
before the insurance pays out?

Take the time to research your pet insurance options.
Compare the different plans available, what each covers,
and the cost before making the decision on which is best for
you and your pet.

Pet insurance may not be the answer for everyone. While it
may not be a feasible option for you, consider having a
backup plan, just in case your cat requires emergency care
or you run into unexpected veterinarian costs.

A simple way to prepare for an emergency is to start a
veterinary fund for your Devon Rex. Decide to put a certain
amount of money aside each week, each month, or each
pay–check to use in the case of an emergency. Think about
the potential financial costs of veterinary care and plan for
how you will pay for it now instead of waiting until
something happens.

Companies in the United States offering pet insurance include:

Healthy Paws
HealthyPawsPetInsurance.com

PetPlan
GoPetPlan.com

Embrace
EmbracePetInsurance.com

Trupanion
Trupanion.com

Pets Best
PetsBest.com

Pet Premium
Enroll.PetPremium.com

The ASPCA
ASPCAPetInsurance.com

PetInsurance
PetInsurance.com

Pet First
PetFirst.com

24PetWatch
24PetWatch.com

Pet insurance companies in the United Kingdom include:

DirectLine
Directline.com/pet-insurance

VetsMediCover
Vetsmedicover.co.uk

PetPlan
Petplan.co.uk

Churchill
Churchill.com/pet-insurance

Animal Friends
Animalfriends.org.uk

Healthy Pets
Healthy-pets.co.uk

For a comprehensive comparison of policies see:
Money.co.uk/pet-insurance.htm

Please note that all companies and links were active at the time of publication in early 2014, but like all Internet content are subject to change. Since pet insurance is growing rapidly in popularity, use the search engine of your choice to look for additional coverage options. Note that the vast majority of sites allow visitors to obtain an estimate price quote online.

Planning for the Unexpected

If something happens to you, you want to know that your cat and any other pets will be properly cared for and loved. Some cell phones allow you to input an ICE (In Case of Emergency) number with notes. If your cell phone has such an option, use it. If it does not, write the following information on a piece of a paper and put it in your wallet with your driver's license:

- The names of each of your pets, including your cat.

- The names and phone numbers of family members or friends who have agreed to temporarily care for your pets in an emergency.

- The name and phone number of your veterinarian.

Be sure to also talk with your neighbors, letting them know how many pets you have and the type of pets. That way, if something happens to you, they can alert the authorities, ensuring your pets do not linger for days before they are found.

If you fail to do that and something happens to you, someone will find your cat and any other pets and will need to know what to do to ensure that they are cared for. It is a good idea in the case of an emergency, to ask several friends or family members to be responsible for taking care of your pets should something happen to you.

Prepare instructions for the intended guardians, providing amended instructions as necessary. Also, be sure to provide each individual with a key to your home (remember to inform your home insurance company so that this does not affect your coverage). Instructions should include:

- The name and phone numbers of each individual who agreed to take care of your cat and other pets.

- Your pet's diet and feeding schedule.

- The name and phone number of your veterinarian.

- Any health problems and medications your cat may take on a daily basis, including dosage instructions, instructions on how to give the medicine, and where the medicine is kept.

Put as much information as necessary to ensure the guardians can provide the same level of care to which your cat is accustomed.

Chapter 7 – To Breed or Not To Breed

Over the years, I have been involved with the breeding of cats. I loved and enjoyed the experience, but I urge you to really think before taking that step. I have seen far too many cases of well-intentioned, enthusiastic people who start a cattery only to experience failure because they weren't truly prepared.

In these cases, the ones who suffer the most are the cats. That is the thing we all want to avoid, and what is always the most heartbreaking for the would-be cat breeder. There's a terrific amount of guilt in the aftermath of a failed breeding operation.

No matter how rewarding you think the project might be, and I assure you can be, it's important that you consider the implications of running a cattery for both you and your family. For this reason, there are a number of things I'd like to suggest that you contemplate fully.

The decision to become a breeder of Devon Rex cats or any other type of cat is one of those choices that may well *sound* better in theory than it plays out to be in reality. With the Devon Rex, there are highly special considerations for mating involving blood type.

It would be highly irresponsible to breed these cats without blood testing and without a clear understanding of other potential genetic defects. Devon Rexes are special cats and require particularly dedicated and knowledgeable cultivation as a breed.

If you are considering becoming a breeder, understand from the beginning that you are not contemplating a mere hobby. Dedicated breeders live and breathe the world of their cats. They share their lives with their cats, or, to put a finer point on it, order their lives according to the needs of their cats.

Also, do not think that becoming a cat breeder is a way to make money. If you have just paid a handsome price for a purebred Devon Rex you may well snort at this assertion in disbelief. Yes, purebred kittens command high prices, but ask any breeder what happens to that money as soon as it comes into their hands.

Their answer will be a firm assurance that the amount goes right back out the door — to pay for vet bills, or cat food, or an addition on the house for the cats or any one of a hundred other cattery related expenses. Breeders who are honest will admit that in a good year, they break even.

There is only one reason to become involved in breeding cats — *love of the breed*.

Questions to Ask Yourself

If you are thinking about becoming a breeder, you need to immerse yourself in the culture of the cat fancy. Attend cat shows and make contact with existing breeders.

When you understand more about cat shows, you'll know that the event itself is not the place to try to have a discussion with a breeder. Instead, use these venues to collect business cards and to see examples of the breed in which you're interested.

Look for local Devon Rex clubs to join, and find online discussion forums to learn more from working breeders. Let me interject a word about forum etiquette. Never just jump into discussions as a "newbie". Spend a few weeks learning the culture of the forum before you post. It is far too easy to give offense without realizing what you are doing.

There are numerous questions you must pose to yourself. The contacts you make and the discussions you have with people knowledgeable about Devon Rex cats and the operation of a cattery will guide you in forming your answers. Be honest with yourself! This is just a short list of things to consider:

- Do you have the time, including nights, weekends, holidays, to devote to the needs of your animals?

- Are you willing to allow your schedule to be dominated — often at a moment's notice — by your cats?

- Are you prepared for the heartache when kittens don't live?

- Are you prepared to see the kittens you have raised go to new homes? No matter how well you screen the adoptive parents or how much money you charge, that is still going to be a painful good-bye.

- Can you cover the initial financial outlay to not only make physical changes to your home, but also to acquire either a high quality queen or a breeding pair?

- Do you live in a setting that is even appropriate for this kind of endeavor? Are there zoning considerations? Homeowners association regulations? Tax implications?

Above all, outline Plan B. Of course you want to go into your new venture with optimism and enthusiasm, but temper that with a healthy dose of realism.

Know what you will do if it all goes wrong. You are bringing living creatures into your care. If you can't sustain the operation of your cattery, what will happen to them?

Memberships

You will gain more information and education from seeking out and joining breed clubs and professional breeder organizations. While there may not be a specific group for every breed, start with a major parent organization like The International Cat Association.

Even if the breed in which you are interested does not have a breeder's association per se, membership in major governing groups will help you to make contact with established breeders and potentially develop a mentoring relationship.

Compiling Estimated Costs

It is almost impossible to know all the costs that might be involved for any one person in setting up a cattery. My best advice to you is to imagine every possible expense and plan for it. Some of the more obvious items on this list should be:

Reference Materials

You are going to need to know everything there is to know about the Devon Rex breed and its genetics. You will need reference materials including subscriptions to feline publications.

Foundation Animals

If you cannot afford a breeding pair, you will at least need a quality queen or stud. You will then need to factor in the cost of pairing your animal with a suitable mate from another cattery.

Veterinary Care

This is obviously a major routine expense for normal health care, but factor in infant and maternal services. Discuss the potential for problem pregnancies with your vet and find out in advance what emergency procedures like C-sections might cost.

You will also have to pay for repeat testing for your queen or stud if they are to go "visit" another cattery. At minimum you will have to produce the results of a recent FELV/FIV test each time.

Equipment, Furniture, Toys

In looking at these expenses, make a complete sub-list and then multiply the costs for everything including, but not limited to: cages, travel crates, play pens, climbing trees, beds and toys.

You will likely be creating an entire cat "room," so think about any kind of furniture you will need or any physical changes to the room that may be required to prevent escapes and enhance its security.

Construction Costs

If you have to add a room on to your house, work with a contractor well in advance of ever purchasing your breeding stock. Everything must be in place before you acquire your cats. If construction costs are prohibitive, this factor alone could derail your plans.

Insurance Considerations

It is impossible to predict the insurance considerations for every individual circumstance. If you are planning to start a cattery, however, a visit with your insurance agent is a must.

You may have to increase your coverage limits or add policy amendments or "riders" to cover additional equipment or square footage and to allow for visitors to your premises.

It is possible that you will also require both liability and indemnity insurance. Work with your agent to determine the appropriate level of coverage for your circumstances and to gain an estimate of the additional premium costs.

Emergency Reserve

It's considered "best practice" to have a 3 - 6 month operating reserve in cash. This is especially crucial if you are put in a position to shut down your operation since you will still have to feed and care for your animals during the time you are placing them in new homes.

Do not proceed without this emergency reserve in place. It's simply not fair to the innocent animals which will be depending on you completely for their well-being.

Going Forward

I've tried to be constructive in laying out some of the challenges and tribulations that will lie ahead of you as I feel it is important to contemplate and reflect on these before taking that big step.

I have seen too many cases of people with the best of intention and enthusiasm start an enterprise only for it to fail due to lack of preparation and thought with the only ones suffering as a result being their cats.

No matter how rewarding you think it might be, it is important that you consider the implications on your lifestyle and that of your family.

If my comments and observations haven't deterred you, then I applaud and welcome you to a most wonderful and challenging pastime which provides so much love and joy. The thrill and sense of achievement you will get from breeding your own Devon Rex cat is one that I know you will cherish and treasure in the years to come.

Chapter 8 – Showing Devon Rex Cats

People who breed Devon Rex cats do so in part to showcase the excellence of their bloodlines, so in this regard, participating in showing is an aspect of their business operations. An impressive collection of awards lends a high degree of prestige to any cattery.

At the same time, however, these people are dedicated proponents of the breeds they cultivate. Remember, however, that if you have purchased a Devon Rex cat from a breeder, you have probably bought a "pet quality" animal. Show quality exemplars of the breed are easily twice the cost.

If you have a show quality cat, there is nothing to keep you from joining the show circuit. The Devon Rex is social, does well with strangers, likes to travel, and is even agreeable to participating in agility contests. He's rather better suited to the show circuit than many other breeds, but this still must be something of a "joint" decision.

You have to decide showing is something you want to do, and then you must judge your pet's suitability to be shown. I am a firm believer that no animal should be made absolutely miserable just to be on a quest for a ribbon.

My best advice to you is to attend cat shows for the purpose of watching and learning. I'm about to run down the basics for you, but you have to experience a show first hand to get even the vaguest sense of the world you're thinking about entering.

The World of the Cat Show

I'm getting ready to give you a lot of information about cat shows, but I want you to hear one thing loudly and clearly from the beginning. When you go to a cat show DO NOT TOUCH THE CATS.

Don't Touch

Yes, you will be in the presence of cats that are physically beautiful and the urge will be overwhelming. Beyond the fact that it's bad manners, you represent a danger to those cats — or more specifically whatever is living on your hands represents a danger.

We walk around with bacteria and viruses on our hands at all times. As already noted, many feline diseases are so contagious all the animals have to do is tap noses to be infected. They don't need our help spreading germs all over their bodies petting them.

And what is the first thing a cat does after a good petting? Licks every hair to get the human scent off. I'm not being facetious. Cats prefer to smell like cats. They like the petting just fine, but they will still groom to make themselves smell the way they think they should.

If you have germs all over your hands, and the cat then licks its fur, the potential for illness is enormous. This is the reason for the "don't touch" rule.

Being invited to touch a cat at a cat show is a huge compliment, one usually extended along with a jar of hand sanitizer. Don't even blink. Use the sanitizer. Do it for the cat.

Don't Help

The second rule after don't touch is don't help. The cry of "loose cat" is heard fairly often in these venues. When a cat makes a break for it, the appropriate thing to do is freeze and be quiet.

Under no circumstances should you join the chase. You'll just frighten the escapee more. If you see the cat, get the attention of the owner and quietly signal where the cat is located.

Get Out of the Way

One thing you do want to do at a cat show is get out of the way. Often you'll hear a rushing exhibitor yell, "Right of way!" That's your cue to yield!

For that matter, don't be surprised if an exhibitor stops talking with you mid-sentence and goes dashing off. When exhibitors are called to the ring, they have only a limited amount of time to get there or be disqualified.

Do not be put off or offended by these instances. Cat shows can be very hectic and chaotic events. Don't contribute to the chaos.

Look and Listen

Remember that you are there to learn. Don't just look at the cats. Observe what's going on. Write down things you want to investigate or questions you want to ask.

Especially when you're near the ring where the judging is going on, be quiet and listen. You'll learn a great deal from the comments the judges make in the ring, and you certainly do not want to distract the exhibitors or the cats.

Cat Show Basics

While this may be the most obvious of statements, a cat show is not a dog show. There are definite differences in how the two kinds of events are run.

For starters, cats are kept secured at all times. Show cats stay in their cages, which are often quite elaborately decorated to call attention to both the animal and the cattery.

This fact lends a festive air to the whole exhibit hall, but the cage rule is strictly a matter of security. The idea is to avoid the "loose cat" situation, although, as we've discussed, that still happens all too often.

A point that is difficult for newbies to grasp is that in terms of movement, cat shows are very, very slow. However, when something is happening, they turn hectic in a heartbeat — like the regular mad dashes to the show ring.

Cat shows include a class for household pets (HHP); dog shows do not. The pet category is responsible for attracting many young people to the cat fancy and is a highly popular part of any show.

Judges evaluate all animals by breed standards formalized by the various agencies responsible for hosting and governing shows. Most of these standards follow or closely resemble the one established by The International Cat Association, which I provide for you later in this chapter.

The various governing bodies for cat shows include:

- The International Cat Association
- Fédération Internationale Féline
- World Cat Federation
- Cat Fanciers Association
- Feline Federation Europe
- Australia Cat Federation
- American Association of Cat Enthusiasts
- American Cat Fanciers Association

Is Showing Right for You and Your Cat?

Before you make the decision to show the Devon Rex, or any other breed for that matter, you have a lot of research to do — on the breed in general, on your cat specifically, on the cat fancy, and on cat shows.

You do not have to participate in the world of the cat fancy to share your life with a beautiful pedigree animal, nor do you have to raise pure bred cats to enjoy their company.

Breeding and showing are pastimes and avocations that should have no other goals but furthering the development of the breed and supporting the welfare of the cats.

Only move forward with showing your cat if you are positive it is the right move for you, but especially, if it is the right move for your cat. If your pet is going to be miserable at a cat show, don't do it. No ribbon is worth that.

Cat Fanciers Association (CFA) Devon Rex Breed Standard

Head	40 Points
Size and Shape	12
Muzzle	5
Profile and Chin	6
Eyes	5
Ears	12
Body	**25 Points**
Torso and Tail	10
Legs and Paws	10
Neck	5
Coat	**30 Points**
Density	10
Texture and Length	10
Waviness	10
Color	**5 Points**

GENERAL: the Devon Rex is a breed of unique appearance. Its large eyes, short muzzle, prominent cheekbones, and huge, low- set ears create a characteristic elfin look. A cat of medium fine frame, the Devon is well covered with soft, wavy fur; the fur is of a distinctive texture, as the mutation which causes its wavy coat is cultivated in no other breed. The Devon is alert and active and shows a lively interest in its surroundings.

HEAD: modified wedge. In the front view, the wedge is delineated by a narrowing series of three distinct convex curves: outer edge of ear lobes, cheekbones, and whisker pads. Head to be broad but slightly longer than it is broad. Face to be full-cheeked with pronounced cheekbones and a whisker break. In profile, nose with a strongly marked stop; forehead curving back to a flat skull. Allowance to be made for stud jowls in the adult male.

MUZZLE: short, well-developed. Prominent whisker pads.

CHIN: strong, well-developed. In profile, chin shall line up vertically with nose, being neither undershot nor overshot.

EYES: large and wide set, oval in shape, and sloping towards outer edges of ears. Any eye color is acceptable, as no points are assigned to eye color (although colorpoints generally will have blue and minks generally will have aqua eyes).

EARS: strikingly large and set very low, very wide at the base, so that the outside base of ear extends beyond the line of the wedge. Tapering to rounded tops and well covered with fine fur. With or without earmuffs and/or ear-tip tufts.

BODY: hard and muscular, lithe, and of medium length. Broad in chest and medium fine in boning, with medium fine but sturdy legs. Carried high on the legs with the hind legs somewhat longer than the front. Allowance to be made for larger size in males, as long as good proportions are maintained.

LEGS and PAWS: legs long and slim. Paws small and oval, with five toes in front and four behind.

TAIL: long, fine, and tapering, well covered with short fur.

NECK: medium long and slender.

COAT: Density: the cat is well covered with fur, with the greatest density occurring on the back, sides, tail, legs, face and ears. Slightly less density is permitted on the top of head, neck, chest and abdomen. Bare patches are a fault in kittens and a serious fault in adults; however the existence of down on the underparts of the body should not be misinterpreted as bareness. Sparse hair on the temples (forehead in front of the ears) is not a fault. **Texture:** the coat is soft, fine, full-bodied, and rexed (i.e. appearing to be without guard hairs). **Length:** the coat is short on the back, sides, upper legs and tail. It is very short on the head, ears, neck, paws, chest and abdomen. Kittens may have very short fur all over; even if not long enough to wave, it must cover the kitten evenly, so that no bare patches are evident. **Waviness:** a rippled wave effect should be apparent when the coat is smoothed with one's hand. The wave is most evident where the coat is the longest, on the body and tail.

PENALIZE: Heads that are long and/or narrow, and/or those tapering in the fashion of a "V"; heads with flared ears; heads that are round, or have the appearance of a mixed breed; extremely short muzzle; misaligned bite;

small or high set ears; short or bare tail; straight coat; bare patches.

DISQUALIFY: extensive baldness, excessively long, and/or shaggy coat; long hair on the tail; kinked or abnormal tail, incorrect number of toes, crossed eyes, weak hind legs; any evidence of illness or poor health.

DEVON REX COLORS

COAT COLOR: any genetically possible color and pattern and any combination of genetically possible color and pattern are allowed.

WHITE: pure glistening white. **Nose leather and paw pads:** pink.

BLACK: dense coal black, sound from roots to tip of fur. Free from any tinge of rust on the tips. **Nose leather:** black. **Paw pads:** black or brown.

BLUE: blue, lighter shade preferred, one level tone from nose to tip of tail. Sound to the roots. A sound darker shade is more acceptable than an unsound lighter shade. **Nose leather and paw pads:** blue.

RED: deep, rich, clear, brilliant red; without shading, markings or ticking. Lips and chin the same color as the coat. **Nose leather and paw pads:** brick red.

CREAM: one level shade of buff cream, without markings. Sound to the roots. Lighter shades preferred. **Nose leather and paw pads:** pink.

CHOCOLATE: rich chestnut brown, sound throughout. **Nose leather:** brown. **Paw pads:** brown or cinnamon.

LAVENDER: frosty-grey with a pinkish tone, sound throughout. **Nose leather and paw pads:** lavender-pink.

CINNAMON: cinnamon, sound throughout. **Nose leather and paw pads:** cinnamon.

FAWN: pale pinkish fawn, sound throughout; lighter shades preferred. **Nose leather and paw pads:** pale fawn.

SHADED PATTERN: undercoat white with a mantle of specified marking color tipping shading down from sides, face and tail from dark on the ridge to white on the chin, chest, stomach and under the tail. Legs to be the same tone as the face. Rims of eyes, lips and nose outlined with marking color. Nose leather and paw pads color as defined below.

SHADED SILVER: Nose leather: brick red. **Paw pads:** black. **BLUE SHADED: Nose leather:** blue or blue with pink tone. **Paw pads:** blue or blue with pink tone.

CHOCOLATE SHADED: Nose leather: pink. **Paw pads:** cinnamon.

LAVENDER SHADED: Nose leather: lavender-pink. **Paw pads:** lavender-pink.

CAMEO SHADED: Nose leather: rose. **Paw pads:** rose.

CREAM SHADED: Nose leather and paw pads: pink.

CINNAMON SHADED: Nose leather: pink. **Paw pads:** coral.

FAWN SHADED: Nose leather: fawn. **Paw pads**: pink.

TORTOISESHELL SHADED: Nose leather and paw pads: as in the solids; may be mottled with pink.

BLUE-CREAM SHADED: Nose leather and paw pads: as in the solids; may be mottled with pink.

CHOCOLATE TORTOISESHELL SHADED: Nose leather and paw pads: as in the solids; may be mottled with pink.

CINNAMON TORTOISESHELL SHADED: Nose leather and paw pads: as in the solids; may be mottled with pink.

LAVENDER-CREAM SHADED: Nose leather and paw pads: as in the solids; may be mottled with pink.

FAWN-CREAM SHADED: Nose leather and paw pads: as in the solids; may be mottled with pink.

CHINCHILLA: undercoat pure white. Coat on back, flanks, head, and tail sufficiently tipped with specified marking color (i.e., black, blue, red, cream, tortoiseshell, etc.) to give the characteristic sparkling appearance. Legs may be slightly shaded with tipping. Chin, stomach and chest, pure white. Rims of eyes, lips and nose outlined with marking color. **Nose leather**: appropriate to pattern and marking color (black/brick red; blue/old rose; red and cream/rose, etc.). **Paw pads**: appropriate to pattern and marking color (black/black; blue/rose; red and cream/rose, etc.).

SMOKE PATTERN: white undercoat more deeply tipped with specified marking color. Cat in repose appears to be of marking color. In motion the white undercoat is apparent.

Points and mask of marking color with narrow band of white at base of hairs next to skin, which may be seen only when fur is parted. **Nose leather and paw pads**: appropriate to pattern and marking color (see below).

BLACK SMOKE: Nose leather and paw pads: black.

BLUE SMOKE: Nose leather and paw pads: blue.

RED SMOKE CAMEO (Cameo): **Nose leather and paw pads**: rose.

CHOCOLATE SMOKE: Nose leather and paw pads: brown or brick.

LAVENDER SMOKE: Nose leather and paw pads: lavender- pink.

CINNAMON SMOKE: Nose leather and paw pads: cinnamon.

CREAM SMOKE: Nose leather and paw pads: pink.

FAWN SMOKE: Nose leather and paw pads: pale fawn.

TORTOISESHELL SMOKE: Nose leather and paw pads: mottled with pink on nose and paws.

BLUE-CREAM SMOKE: Nose leather and paw pads: mottled with pink on nose and paws.

CHOCOLATE TORTOISESHELL SMOKE: Nose leather and paw pads: mottled with pink on nose and paws.

LAVENDER-CREAM SMOKE: Nose leather and paw pads: mottled with pink on nose and paws.

CINNAMON TORTOISESHELL SMOKE: Nose leather and paw pads: mottled with pink on nose and paws.

FAWN-CREAM SMOKE: Nose leather and paw pads: pink.

CLASSIC TABBY PATTERN: markings dense, clearly defined, and broad. Legs evenly barred with bracelets coming up to meet the body markings. Tail evenly ringed. Several unbroken neck- laces on neck and upper chest, the more the better. Frown marks on forehead form an intricate letter "M." Unbroken line runs back from outer corner of eye. Swirls on cheeks. Vertical lines over back of head extend to shoulder markings, which are in the shape of a butterfly with both upper and lower wings distinctly outlined and marked with dots inside outline. Back markings consist of a vertical line down the spine from butterfly to tail with a vertical stripe paralleling it on each side, the three stripes well separated by stripes of the ground color. Large solid blotch on each side to be encircled by one or more unbroken rings. Side markings should be the same on both sides. Double vertical rows of buttons on chest and stomach.

MACKEREL TABBY PATTERN: markings dense, clearly defined, and all narrow pencillings. Legs evenly barred with narrow bracelets coming up to meet the body markings. Tail barred. Necklaces on neck and chest distinct, like so many chains. Head barred with an "M" on the forehead. Unbroken lines running back from the eyes. Lines running down the head to meet the shoulders. Spine lines run together to form a narrow saddle. Narrow pencillings run around body.

SPOTTED TABBY PATTERN: markings on the body to be spot- ted. The spots can be round, oblong, or rosette-shaped. Any of these are of equal merit but the spots, however shaped or placed, shall be distinct. Spots should not run together in a broken Mackerel pattern. A dorsal stripe runs the length of the body to the tip of the tail. The stripe is ideally composed of spots. The markings on the face and forehead shall be typically tabby markings. Underside of the body to have "vest buttons." Legs and tail are barred.

TICKED TABBY PATTERN: body hairs to be ticked with various shades of marking color and ground color. Body when viewed from top to be free from noticeable spots, stripes, or blotches, except for darker dorsal shading. Lighter underside may show tabby markings. Face, legs and tail must show distinct tabby striping. Cat must have at least one distinct necklace.

PATCHED TABBY PATTERN: a patched tabby (torbie) is an established silver, brown, blue, lavender, fawn, cinnamon or chocolate tabby with patches of red or cream clearly defined on both the body and extremities; a blaze on the face is desirable.

SILVER TABBY: ground color, including lips and chin, pale clear silver. Markings dense black. **Nose leather:** brick red. **Paw pads:** black.

BROWN TABBY: ground color brilliant coppery brown. Markings dense black. Lips and chin the same shade as the rings around the eyes. Back of leg black from paw to heel. **Nose leather:** brick red. **Paw pads:** black or brown.

BLUE TABBY: ground color, including lips and chin, pale bluish ivory. Markings a very deep blue affording a good contrast with ground color. Warm fawn overtones or patina over the whole. **Nose leather:** old rose. **Paw pads:** rose.

RED TABBY: ground color red. Markings deep, rich red. Lips and chin red. **Nose leather and paw pads:** brick red.

CREAM TABBY: ground color, including lips and chin, very pale cream. Markings buff or cream sufficiently darker than the ground color to afford good contrast but remaining within the dilute color range. **Nose leather and paw pads:** pink.

CHOCOLATE (Chestnut) TABBY: ground color is warm fawn, markings are rich chestnut brown. **Nose leather:** chestnut, or pink rimmed with chestnut. **Paw pads:** cinnamon.

CHOCOLATE SILVER TABBY: ground color, including lips and chin, is silver. Markings rich chestnut. **Nose leather:** chestnut or pink rimmed with chestnut. **Paw pads:** cinnamon.

CINNAMON TABBY: ground color, including lips and chin, a pale, warm honey, markings a dense cinnamon, affording a good contrast with ground color. **Nose leather:** cinnamon or coral rimmed with cinnamon. **Paw pads:** cinnamon.

CINNAMON SILVER TABBY: ground color, including lips and chin, a pale glistening silver. Markings dense cinnamon. **Nose leather:** cinnamon. **Paw pads:** coral.

LAVENDER TABBY: ground color is pale lavender. Markings are a rich lavender, affording a good contrast with ground color. **Nose leather:** lavender, or pink rimmed with lavender. **Paw pads:** lavender-pink.

LAVENDER SILVER TABBY: ground color, including lips and chin, a cold clear silver. Markings sound lavender. **Nose leather:** lavender or pink rimmed with lavender. **Paw pads:** lavender-pink.

FAWN TABBY: ground color, including lips and chin, pale ivory, markings dense fawn, affording good contrast with ground color. **Nose leather and paw pads:** pale fawn.

CAMEO TABBY: ground color off-white. Markings red. **Nose leather and paw pads:** rose.

BLUE SILVER, CREAM SILVER, and FAWN SILVER TABBIES: tabby pattern with colors and leathers same as for corresponding shaded colors.

TORTOISESHELL: black mottled or patched with areas of red or shades of red. Presence of several shades of red acceptable.

BLUE-CREAM: blue mottled or patched with cream. Blaze on face is desirable.

CHOCOLATE (Chestnut) TORTOISESHELL: rich chestnut brown mottled or patched with red or shades of red. Presence of several shades of red acceptable.

CINNAMON TORTOISESHELL: cinnamon mottled or patched with red or shades of red. Presence of several shades of red acceptable.

LAVENDER-CREAM: lavender mottled or patched with cream. Blaze on face desirable.

FAWN-CREAM: fawn mottled or patched with cream. Blaze on face desirable.

CALICO: white with unbrindled patches of black and red. White pre-dominant on underparts.

VAN CALICO: white cat with unbrindled patches of black and red confined to the extremities; head, tail, legs. One or two small patches of color on body allowable.

DILUTE CALICO: white with unbrindled patches of blue and cream. White predominant on underparts.

DILUTE VAN CALICO: white cat with unbrindled patches of blue and cream confined to the extremities; head, tail, legs. One or two small patches of color on body allowable.

BI-COLOR: solid color and white, tabby and white, tortoiseshell and white, etc.

VAN BI-COLOR: solid color and white, tabby and white, tortoise- shell and white, etc., with color confined to the extremities; head, tail, and legs. One or two small patches on body allowable.

FAWN CALICO, LAVENDER CALICO, CHOCOLATE CALICO and CINNAMON CALICO: as for CALICO above, with appropriate marking color.

FAWN VAN CALICO, LAVENDER VAN CALICO, CHOCOLATE VAN CALICO and CINNAMON VAN

CALICO: as for VAN CALI- CO above, with appropriate marking color.

POINTED PATTERN: body color lighter, with some color allowed. Allowance to be made for darker body color in older cats, but contrast between points and body must be evident. **Points:** mask, ears, legs, tail and feet clearly defined. Mask should not extend over the top of the head. **Nose leather and paw pads:** appropriate to coat color. The pointed pattern may be combined with ANY other pattern (except mink) and ANY colors, e.g. lilac-silver lynx point and seal-tortie point with white (shown in the Bi-Color Class).

MINK PATTERN: body with some color. Contrast between body color and points ranging from subtle to distinct in kittens and young cats. Contrast minimal in older cats, particularly in darker colors, tabbies and torties. **Points:** mask, ears, legs, tail and feet with even color. **Nose leather and paw pads:** appropriate to coat color. **Eye color:** aqua. The mink pattern may be combined with ANY other pattern (except pointed or sepia) and ANY colors, e.g. natural mink, blue mink, champagne mink, platinum mink, cinnamon mink, fawn mink, red mink, cream mink, natural tabby mink, blue-cream mink, tortie mink, platinum-smoke mink, etc., or combined with red in dominant colors and cream in recessive colors, smoke, shaded, and tabby patterns, all shown in the ODRC class. Any color and pattern, when combined with white, is shown in the Bi-color class.

SEPIA PATTERN: the mature cat should be rich and even in color, shading almost imperceptibly to a slightly lighter hue on the under parts. Kittens are often lighter in color. **Nose leather and paw pads:** appropriate to coat color. **Eye color:** yellow/gold to green. The sepia pattern may be combined with ANY other pattern (except pointed or mink) and ANY colors, e.g. sable sepia, blue sepia, champagne sepia, platinum sepia, cinnamon sepia, fawn sepia, red sepia, cream sepia, etc., or combined with red in dominant colors and cream in recessive colors, smoke, shaded, and tabby patterns, all shown in the ODRC class. Any color and pattern, when combined with white, is shown in the Bi-color class.

ODRC (Other Devon Rex Colors): any other color or pattern. Cats with no more than a locket and/or button do not qualify for this class, such cats shall be judged in the color class of their basic color with no penalty for such locket and/or button. Examples: smoke pattern, all point restricted colors such as seal point, chocolate point, blue point, lilac point, cream point, lynx points, cinnamon point, etc.

Chapter 9 – Care Sheet

A fter reading this book, you may feel overwhelmed by the sheer volume of the information covered. For a quick reference to key information about Devon Rex cats as detailed in this book, check the summaries included in this care sheet:

Physical Characteristics

Size: Medium.

Build: Solid and muscular

Weight: 6 - 9 lbs. / 2.73 – 4.08 kg

Coat Length: Short/medium, pronounced curls and waves

Colors: All colors, patterns and markings accepted.

Lifespan: 9 - 15 years

Grooming

Minimal: Due to the fragility of the coat, brushing and combing is not recommended. Beyond regular claw clipping and basic at-home ear care (not the inner ear), the occasional cleaning with a warm, damp cloth is all that is needed.

Personality

The Devon Rex is active, social, engaged and participatory. These cats do well with other pets regardless of species, and get along well with children in family situations. They do require the time and attention of their humans, and do not like to be left alone for extended periods of time.

Food and Water for Adults

Dry Food – Give a quarter to half a cup per day or 2 to 4 ounces / 56.7 to 113 grams.

Wet food – Give approximately 5.5 ounces / 156 grams once to twice daily.

Provide a constant source of clean fresh water.

Litter Box

Ensure the texture of litter and type of box are to the cat's preference, making certain to scoop it out daily and changed out completely 1 - 2 times per week.

Health Care

Initial spaying or neutering with regular program of vaccinations in consultation with a qualified veterinarian. General preventive health care including dental. See the chapter on health for a complete discussion of potential genetic health issues.

Chapter 10 – Closing Thoughts

The Devon Rex is a hard cat to commit to paper. He has to be seen and experienced in person. In my case, it was grand muffin larceny that set me on the path to falling in love with the breed. Devons are not conventional cats, either in appearance or behavior. They're not for everyone, but for the people who do love them, Devons are exceptional companions.

I've never seen one refuse a meal or a lap or fail to offer an opinion on whatever you're doing, from filing your taxes to hanging the Christmas lights. If they're not in your lap, they're perched on your shoulder. All the world is a cat toy in a Devon's eyes and every activity has the potential to be a game, after all, what else could you possibly have to do with your time?

Don't even think about getting a Devon Rex if you don't have the time to spend with him. And go ahead and buy an extra pillow, because he'll move into your bed the first night and be there for life. This is a breed that is omnipresent and super devoted. I really can't say enough about their capacity to love their humans, or their boundless streams of playful energy.

I don't recommend that anyone but the most expert cat owners attempt to breed the Devon Rex. There are serious genetic considerations, which I discuss in the chapter on health, but I do heartily recommend these fine fellows as housemates and best friends. They're one of my favorite breeds and will be one of yours in no time.

Chapter 11 – Relevant Websites

The Cat Fanciers Association, Inc.
www.cfainc.org/Breeds/

CFA Devon Rex Breed Profile
www.cfainc.org/Breeds/BreedsCJ/DevonRex.aspx

The Devon Zone
www.devonzone.net

Devon Rex Breed Club
www.devonrexbreedclub.com

Devon Rex – Euro Cat Fancy
www.eurocatfancy.de/ru1/nav/cat-breeds/DRX/devonrex_profile.html

PetMD – Devon Rex
www.petmd.com/cat/breeds/c_ct_devon_rex

Rex Cat Association
www.rexcatassociation.co.uk

Rex Cat Club
www.rexcatclub.com

Rex Cat Club of N.S.W.
rexcatclub.tripod.com

Russian Devon Rex Club
www.devonrexclub.ru/eng/

Scottish Rex Cat Club
www.ursus.clara.net/devonrex.html

VetStreet Devon Rex Profile
www.vetstreet.com/cats/devon-rex

United States

"Feeding Your Adult Cat." The American Society for the Prevention of Cruelty to Animals.
www.aspca.org/pet-care/cat-care/nutrition-tips-adult-cat.aspx

"Nutrition for the Adult Cat." Virginia-Maryland Regional College of Veterinary Medicine.

www.vetmed.vt.edu/vth/sa/clin/cp_handouts/Nutrition_A
dult_Cat.pdf

"Nutritional Requirements and Related Diseases of Small
Animals." The Merck Veterinary Manual.
www.merckmanuals.com/vet/management_and_nutrition/
nutrition_small_animals/nutritional_requirements_and_rel
ated_diseases_of_small_animals.html

United Kingdom

"Cat Nutrition." LondonVet Clinic.
www.londonvetclinic.co.uk/advice.aspx?a=1100&clientId=2
0138

"Cat Nutrition." Moggies.co.uk.
www.moggies.co.uk/articles/nutrition.html

"Cat Nutrition." Hornsey VETS.
hornseyvets.co.uk/preventative-care/cat-nutrition.php

"Cat Health and Welfare." The Royal Society for the
Prevention of Cruelty to Animals.
www.rspca.org.uk/allaboutanimals/pets/cats/health

"Cat Health Information." The CornYard Veterinary
Centre.
www.cornyardvets.co.uk/cat.html

"Cat Health." Chase View Veterinary Clinic.
www.chaseviewvets.co.uk/cat-health/

Shopping

www.PamperedCatShop.com

www.PamperedCatShop.co.uk

Chapter 12 – Frequently Asked Questions

While I recommend that you read the entire text to get a good sense of life with a Devon Rex, for those of you who like to get a "quick start" on a subject, these are some of the most frequently asked questions I encounter about this breed.

Why is the Devon Rex so popular?

Many people are initially attracted to the unique look of the Devon Rex, both in terms of its curly coat and its elfin, pixie-like features. In truth, however, once you really come to know the personality-tour-de-force of a Devon, there's no going back.

These are some of the most devoted, loyal, affectionate and

interactive cats on the planet. If you have the time and attention to give a Devon, he will reward you with a quality of feline friendship that will both astound and delight you.

What should I look for in selecting a Devon Rex kitten?

Generally Devon Rex kittens that are offered for adoption are at least 16 weeks of age. They should be happy and interested, with only a little initial shyness. There should be no discharge from the eyes and ears, and the ears should be clean with no odor.

Healthy kittens have soft, shiny fur Even though many Devons have very thin, fine, "suede-like" coats, there should not be any bald spots. The body should feel solid and healthy, not bony. Good hydration should be evident in the gums, which should be pink and moist.

What's the best way to find a good breeder?

One of the best ways to get in touch with high-quality breeders is to attend cat shows. Catteries exhibit their finest animals at these venues and, while you cannot adopt on the spot, you can collect business cards.

Do Devon Rex need any kind of special diet?

Any cat may need a special diet to help in the management of a health condition, but most cats, including Devon Rex, thrive on a balanced and varied diet of high-quality wet and dry foods. You do have to be very careful to feed your Devon a fixed amount on a set schedule. These cats are absolute chowhounds and consummate beggars. You can't let them have their way at the dinner table – theirs or yours!

How much grooming is required for a Devon Rex cat?

Beyond the occasional wipe-down with a damp washrag, claw clipping, and basic at-home ear care (not the inner ear), there are no grooming requirements for this breed. Given the fragility of their coat, combing and brushing is not recommended.

Will my Devon Rex shed more seasonally?

Really any breed of cat will shed more in the summer months, but since Devons barely shed at all, you will likely not notice any difference. Some individuals do molt or lose their entire coats before two-years of age, but otherwise there's very little cast off hair with this breed.

Is there any difference in temperament and adaptability in a male or female Devon Rex?

The gender question really isn't a huge concern in my opinion. All cats are individuals with unique personalities. Cats, like people, develop in response to their life experiences. I've had cats of many breeds of both genders. I've rarely found gender to be an absolute indicator of personality.

Is there a problem with a male Devon Rex spraying?

I have never had an issue with male cats of any breed spraying, regardless of their intact or altered status. The behavior is even less likely in neutered males.

The neutering surgery is performed before six months of age. At that stage, the cats are just too young to start spraying.

Female cats can spray as well, although they do so only rarely. I think it's fair to say that well cared for, happy, healthy cats don't display problem behavior of any kind, including spraying.

The spraying stereotype is, in my opinion, unfairly applied to male cats. If it does happen, it likely indicates a cat that is either unhappy or physically ill.

Appendix 1 – Devon Rex Cat Breeders List

I've put together a list of breeders but I don't approve or endorse any as they are just meant to be an aid in locating one near you. You may be interested in this site for further details: http://planetdevon.com/breeders

United States

Alabama
Gaia
Sue Perkins
gaia_devons@yahoo.com
www.gaiadevonrex.blogspot.com

Steadham Cats
256-473-8856
Madison, AL
steadhamcats@gmail.com
www.steadhamcats.com

Arizona
DevineDevons
Desert Hills, AZ
Robin Robertson
623-376-9721
robin@devinedevons.com

California
ElfinKurl Devon Rex
Diane Jackson
818-929-6937 cell
www.elfinkurl.com

L.A. Devons
C. Orlinsky
http://ladevons.wix.com/cattery#!__devons

Pattnchat
Debbie Van Patten
pattnchat@aol.com
www.pattnchat.wordpress.com

Permarex Cattery
Anita Henrikson
www.permarex.com/index.html

Colorado
Curly Dolls
Dolly Chamness
curlydolls@gmail.com
719-207-4257
https://sites.google.com/site/curlydolls/home

Florida
Ciandor
Meaghan Morriseau
ciandor.info@gmail.com
www.ciandor.com

Nada
Cheryl Kerr
www.sphynx.us.com

Georgia
JG Whiskerz
Jennifer and Glenn Viveiros
www.facebook.com/pages/JG-Whiskerz-Devon-Rex/236025196426149

Illinois
Autumn Rain
Denise Blacker
www.rexkittensforsale.com

Jedi Devons
Heather Roozee
graco22@aol.com
www.facebook.com/pages/Jedi-Devon-Rex-Cats/103927547524?sk=timeline

Whiskerbreak
John Baietti
realnchgo@aol.com

Indiana
Meikai
Douglas Schmidt
Schmidt4Marken@aol.com
219-785-4238

Iowa
Everafter
Tina Chittick
everafterdevons@aol.com
319 363-7343

Louisiana
CheriBebe Cattery
Marilyn Cooley, Jennifer Cooley
mari6607@hotmail.com; jennifercooley80@hotmail.com
318-715-6277 cell 318-880-3898

Massachusetts
Talegre
Tony Costa
tonycosta01@aol.com
(781) 279-3523

Michigan
Elvendom
Evelyn Dominguez
egnelson21@gmail.com

Minnesota
Barashta
Rebecca Ansari
TealAndCobalt@netzero.net

New York
HostaHaven Devon Rex
Wendy Garcia
www.facebook.com/HostaHavenDevonRex

North Carolina
Kurakats.com
Fleetwood, NC
Lisa Seay
ramses@kurakats.com
336-877- 2248

Oregon
Happy Tales
Teresa Haro
www.happytalescattery.com

Texas
Tx-Elfkatz
Deer Park, TX
Michelle Piatt
www.tx-elfkatz.com/index.html

Utah
Jobara Devons
Barbara Irie and Jade Kleider
www.jobara-devons-exotics.com
jobara@comcast.net

Nu Moon Cattery
Tina Orfanos
tinaspets64@hotmail.com
www.numooncattery.com

Virgina
Karmacatz
Linda Peterson
www.catterysites.com/Karmacatz

Washington

Bat Cave
Mel MacPherson
melissa@batcavecattery.com

FaceHuggers
Lyssa Paull and Trisha Durdy
manxtek@gmail.com
http://manxtech.tripod.com/Faerietail.html

Movieland Cattery
Jeannie Kelley
www.movielandcattery.com

RainingRexes
Mary Ann Gobat
maryann@rainingrexes.com
253 529-8969 or 253 529-9126

Storybook
Doug and Mika Day
storybookdevon@gmail.com
www.storybookdevon.com

United Kingdom

Below is just a sample list of available breeders. A full list of Breeders can be found at: www.rexcatclub.com/breeders-list.html

Essex
Akatofarr Devon Rex
Mrs. Jenny Morris
merseateazle@aol.com
Tel. 01206 384660

Galloway
Glenkens Birmans and Devon Rexes
Mrs. Anne Mellor
annemellor387@btinternet.com
www.glenkensbirmansanddevonrexes.co.uk

Grimsby
Rascalirex Devon Rex
Mrs. A. Christoffersen
Tel. 01472 877405

Hampshire
Stickybicky Devon Rex
Mr. & Mrs. Laurence & Jane Keates
lmkeates@aol.com
Tel. 02380 403436

Kent
Yassassin Devon Rex
Nikki Fereday
nikkicatcrazy@aol.co.uk
www.yassassindevonrex.com

Lancashire
Amun Devon Rex
Mrs. Barbara Rehman
barbara.rehman@sky.com
Tel. 07872 190169
www.amuncats.wordpress.com

Manchester
Mrs. Audrey Y. Shepherd
audreyshepherd@virginmedia.com
Tel. 0161 371 7177
audreyshepherd.wix.com/magical-devon-rex

Mid Glamorgan
Lexifers Devon Rex
Mrs. Sarah Morgan
lexifers@talktalk.net
Tel. 01443 225373
www.lexifersdevonrex.co.uk

North Staffordshire/Cheshire
Nidoran Devon Rex
Mrs. Kath Wilson and Mike Wilson
kathwilson-nidoran@hotmail.com
Tel. 01782 771172
www.nidorancattery.co.uk

Nottingham
Karenanne Devon Rex
Mrs. A. Hawthorn & Mrs. K. Kindell
kindellkaren@yahoo.com
Tel. 0115 933 2940
www.karenannedevonrexcats.co.uk

Nottinghamshire
Onaway Devon Rex
Mrs. Diana Read
c.read4@ntworld.com
Tel. 01623 489969
www.onawaydevons.co.uk

Ripplerex Devon Rex
Mrs. Linda Foster
rexylindy@aol.com
Tel. 0115 962 0041
www.ripplerexdevonrex.com

Swansea
Amourex Devon Rex
Mrs. Rosalind Davis
rosalind_davies2000@yahoo.co.uk
Tel. 01792 297191

Wetherby
Peppadora Devon Rex
Mrs. Adele Almond
peppadoradevens@aol.com
Tel. 07866 283162

West Midlands
Maystar Devon Rex
Mrs. Nicole SJ Rankin
rankinn@hotmail.com
Tel. 07857 617263
www.maystardevonrex.co.uk

Rexiru Devon Rex
Miss Emma J. Warrener
emma.warrener@sky.com
Tel. 02476 581376
www.rexiru.co.uk

Appendix 2 – Toxic Plants List

The following is a fairly comprehensive though not exhaustive list but please check with your breeder or veterinarian for dangerous plants and flowers in your area.

Almond (pits)

Aloe Vera

Alocasia

Amaryllis

American Yew

Apple (seeds)

Apple Leaf Croton

Apricot (pits)

Arrowgrass

Asparagus Fern

Autumn Crocus

Avocado (fruit and pit)

Azalea Baby's Breath

Baneberry

Bayonet

Beargrass

Beech

Belladonna

Bird of Paradise

Bittersweet

Black-eyed Susan

Black Locust

Bleeding Heart

Bloodroot

Bluebonnet

Box

Boxwood

Branching Ivy

Buckeyes

Buddhist Pine

Burning Bush

Buttercup Cactus

Candelabra

Caladium

Calla Lily

Castor Bean

Ceriman

Charming Dieffenbachia

Cherry (pits, seeds, leaves)

Cherry Laurel

Chinaberry

Chinese Evergreen

Christmas Rose

Chrysanthemum

Cineria

Clematis

Cordatum

Coriaria

Cornflower

Corn Plant

Cornstalk Plant

Croton

Corydalis

Crocus, Autumn

Crown of Thorns

Cuban Laurel

Cutleaf Philodendron

Cycads

Cyclamen

Daffodil

Daphne	English Yew
Datura	Eucalyptus
Deadly Nightshade	Euonymus
Death Camas	Evergreen Ferns
Devil's Ivy	Fiddle-leaf Fig
Delphinium	Florida Beauty
Decentrea	Flax
Dieffenbachia	Four O'Clock
Dracaena Palm	Foxglove
Dragon Tree	Fruit Salad Plant
Dumb Cane	Geranium
Easter Lily	German Ivy
Eggplant	Giant Dumb Cane
Elaine	Glacier Ivy
Elderberry	Golden Chain
Elephant Ear	Gold Dieffenbachia
Emerald Feather	Gold Dust Dracaena
English Ivy	Golden Glow

Golden Pothos

Gopher Purge

Hahn's Self-Branching Ivy

Heartland Philodendron

Hellebore

Hemlock, Poison

Hemlock, Water

Henbane

Holly

Horsebeans

Horsebrush

Hellebore

Horse Chestnuts

Hurricane Plant

Hyacinth

Hydrangea

Indian Rubber Plant

Indian Tobacco

Iris

Iris Ivy

Jack in the Pulpit

Janet Craig Dracaena

Japanese Show Lily

Java Beans

Jessamine

Jerusalem Cherry

Jimson Weed

Jonquil

Jungle Trumpets

Kalanchoe

Lacy Tree Philodendron

Lantana

Larkspur

Laurel

Lily

Lily Spider

Lily of the Valley	Narcissus
Locoweed	Needlepoint Ivy
Lupine	Nephytis
Madagascar Dragon Tree	Nightshade Oleander
Marble Queen	Onion
Marigold	Oriental Lily
Marijuana	Peace Lily
Mescal Bean	Peach (pits and leaves)
Mexican Breadfruit	Pencil Cactus
Miniature Croton	Peony
Mistletoe	Periwinkle
Mock Orange	Philodendron
Monkshood	Pimpernel
Moonseed	Plumosa Fern
Morning Glory	Poinciana
Mother-in-Law's Tongue	Poinsettia (low toxicity)
Mountain Laurel	Poison Hemlock
Mushrooms	Poison Ivy

Poison Oak	Satin Pathos
Pokeweed	Schefflera
Poppy	Scotch Broom
Potato	Silver Pothos
Pothos	Skunk Cabbage
Precatory Bean	Snowdrops
Primrose	Snow on the Mountain
Privet, Common	Spotted Dumb Cane
Red Emerald	Staggerweed
Red Princess	Star of Bethlehem
Red-Margined Dracaena	String of Pearls
Rhododendron	Striped Dracaena
Rhubarb	Sweetheart Ivy
Ribbon Plan	Sweetpea
Rosemary Pea	Swiss Cheese plant
Rubber Plant	Tansy Mustard
Saddle Leaf Philodendron	Taro Vine
Sago Palm	Tiger Lily

Tobacco

Tomato Plant (green fruit, stem, leaves)

Tree Philodendron

Tropic Snow Dieffenbachia

Tulip

Tung Tree

Virginia Creeper

Water Hemlock

Weeping Fig

Wild Call

Western Yew

Wisteria Yews

Yew, American

Yew, English

Yew, Western

Yew, Wisteria

Source: The Cat Fancier's Association, CFA.org/CatCare/HouseholdHazards/ToxicPlants.aspx

Glossary

A

Ailurophile – One who loves and is actively involved with cats. Also a committed member of the cat fancy.

Ailurophobe – Any person who harbors a dislike of cats or who has a fear of cats. This can be in response to a bad experience, a simple expression of preference, or an actual phobia.

Allergen – The primary allergen in cats is the protein Fel d 1, which is produced by the animal's saliva and sebaceous glands. In people with sensitivity, Fel d 1 triggers a pronounced allergic reaction.

Allergy – An allergy is a pronounced sensitivity to an environmental agent that triggers a cascade of responses in a sensitive person including, but not limited to, sneezing, watering eyes, itching and skin rashes.

Alter – An accepted term indicating that a cat or dog has been neutered or spayed and thus made incapable of reproduction. A similar, colloquial term frequently used with the same meaning is "fixed".

B

Bloodline – In pedigreed cats, the bloodline is the animal's verifiable line of descent. It is used for the purposes of establishing pedigree.

Breed Standard – Feline governing organizations publish established sets of standards outline the points considered necessary for an individual animal to be regarded as a perfect example of any given breed. The standards are used for the purpose of judging at cat shows.

Breed – Any group of cats with a defined set of physical characteristics that are reliably passed on to subsequent generations and that distinguish them from other types of cats is said to be a distinct "breed".

Breeder - A breeder is a person who works with male and female cats of a particular breed, pairing the animals to produce offspring that exhibit exceptionally high quality according to the accepted standards for the type of cat in question.

Breeding - In the sense of an organized promulgation of a breed within the cat fancy, breeding is the process whereby sires and dams are paired with an eye toward the superior quality of their offspring.

Breeding Program – A breeding program is an organized effort to selectively breed superior individuals of any type of cat for the express purpose of producing offspring of exceptional quality.

Breeding Quality – A cat is said to be of breeding quality when it exhibits sufficiently superior traits according to the accepted breed standard to be regarded as suitable for participation in an organized breeding program.

Breed True – When cats of the same breed pass on an identifiable set of physical characteristics from one generation to the next, those traits are said to "breed true". These might include such things as coat color or type, eye color, or physical conformation.

C

Carpal Pads - A cat's carpal pads are found on the animal's front legs at the "wrists". These pads serve to provide additional traction to the animal when walking.

Castrate – Castration is the medical procedure for the removal of a male cat's testicles to render the animal incapable of reproduction.

Caterwaul - A caterwaul is a high-pitched and strident feline vocalization that is discordant and unpleasant.

Cat Fancy – The "cat fancy" is comprised of those individuals actively interested in breeding, showing, and even simply appreciating cats of various breeds and types as well as the registered associations and clubs to which they belong.

Catnip – Catnip is a perennial herb in the mint family. Its scientific name is *Nepeta cataria*. Many cats are strongly attracted to catnip and exhibit mild intoxication upon contact with it. Kittens cannot experience this response, however, until they are at least 6-9 months of age.

Cattery – A cattery is any establishment where cats are housed, usually as part of an organized program of breeding.

Certified Pedigree – Certified pedigrees are issued by feline registering associations and are a validation of an individual animal's genetic authenticity as a prime example of a given breed.

Clowder – Clowder is a collective name indicating a group of cats gathered in one place at one time.

Coat – Coat is the accepted term used in reference to a cat's fur. The major qualifiers in this regard are long and shorthaired.

Crate – Any small container that can be securely locked and that is used to temporarily confine a cat or other companion animal for the purposes of safe transport is referred to as a "crate".

Crepuscular – Animals that exhibit crepuscular behavior are most active at dawn and dusk, which is the accurate term for the most active periods in a cat's day. It is not correct to say that these animals are nocturnal, even though they do possess excellent low light vision.

Crossbred – Any cat that is the product of a mating between a dam and a sire of different breeds is crossbred. This may occur as an accident or as an intentional effort to create a new and distinct breed exhibiting desirable qualities of the two foundation breeds.

D

Dam – In a mating pair of cats, the female is often referred to as the "dam".

Dander – Dander refers to the small scales that are shed along with the hair of an animal that are often created by saliva that dried on the fur as a consequence of self-grooming. Dander plays a leading role in the triggering of allergic reactions in people with specific sensitivity. In cats, the presence of the protein Fel d 1 in the dander is mainly responsible for this reaction in humans.

Declawing – Declawing is an extremely controversial surgical procedure in which the last digit of the cat's toes are removed so that the animal is permanently deprived of its claws. In theory the procedure developed as an anti-scratching measure, but it is now seen as excessive and cruel and is illegal in Europe and many parts of the United States.

Desex – "Desexing" is an accepted term to describe the procedures, either spaying or neutering, whereby animals are deprived of their ability to reproduce.

Domesticated – Domesticated animals are those creatures that, through long association, have come to be tame and to live in companionship with humans either to work or to serve as companions.

E

Ear Mites – Ear mites are microscopic parasites often present in the ear canals of felines. They cause redness and irritation, leading to an accumulation of black, tarry debris and often secondary yeast infections. This is an extremely unpleasant infestation for the cat accompanied by extreme itching. It is detectable not only by the visible inflammation, but also by the presence of a strong and unpleasant odor.

Entire – Entire is a term used in the cat fancy to describe an animal that has not been spayed or neutered and therefore has an intact reproductive system.

Exhibitor – An exhibitor is an individual who participates in a cat show either with a cat he or she owns or as a representative of the owner.

F

Fel d 1 – The protein Fel d 1 can be found in the sebaceous glands and saliva of cats. It is responsible for causing an allergic reaction in humans who have a specific sensitivity to it. This reaction includes, but is not limited so, sneezing, watering eyes, nasal congestion and itching.

Feline - A feline is any animal that is a member of the family Felidae. This group includes "big" cats like lions, tigers, and jaguars, as well as domestic cats.

Fleas – Fleas are parasites of the order Siphonaptera that feed on the blood of the host animal they infest. These creatures do not have wings, but are well adapted to jump.

Flehmening/Flehmen Reaction – In cats, the Flehmen Reaction is often mistaken as a facial grimace indicating dislike. In reality, this "expression" during which the cat holds its mouth partially open is adopted for the express purpose of allowing air to pass over a special structure in the roof of the mouth just behind the upper front teeth called Jacobsen's Organ. The organ, which is two small holes, functions as a secondary set of nostrils giving the cat the ability to essentially "taste" a scent or odor.

G

Gene pool – The gene pool in any population of organisms refers to the collective genetic information of the group relative to its diversity and reproduction.

Genes – Genes are the distinct hereditary units responsible for specific characteristics passed down from one generation of organisms to another. Genes consist of a DNA sequence found at a specific location on a chromosome.

Genetic – The term genetics is used in reference to any inherited trait or characteristic identifiable from one generation to the next.

Genetically Linked Defects – Any specific health or physical problem passed from one generation to the next that is, in some way, negative, harmful, or potentially limiting in nature.

Genetics – Genetics is the scientific study of heredity.

Genotype – A genotype is the term referring to the genetic makeup of an organism or a group of organisms.

Groom – Grooming refers to the procedures and protocols involved in caring for the coat of a cat including, but not limited to brushing, combing, trimming or washing.

Guard Hair – Guard hairs are longer, coarser hairs that form the outer or top layer of the coat on some breeds of cat.

H

Heat – "Heat" is the commonly accepted term to designate when a female cat reaches the point in seasonal estrus when she is ready to be impregnated by a male.

Hereditary – Hereditary elements including traits, diseases, or conditions are genetically transmitted from parents to their offspring.

Histamine - Histamines are physiologically active amines present in plant and animal tissue that are released from musk cells as part of an allergic reaction.

Hock – In anatomical nomenclature, a hock is that part of a cat's hind leg we would describe as the animal's "ankle".

Housetraining – Housetraining or housebreaking is the process of training a cat to live cleanly in a home with humans utilizing a litter box or pan.

Humane Societies – Humane societies are, in a general sense, groups working to end animal suffering as a consequence of overt cruelty, impoverishment or similar circumstances. The umbrella organization in the United States is The Humane Society of the United States and in the United Kingdom it is Humane Society International.

I

Immunization – Immunization is the targeted use of injections for the purpose of cultivating immunity against disease. The injections are also commonly called vaccinations.

Innate – When a quality, tendency or trait is said to be innate, it has been present since birth.

Inbreeding – The act of inbreeding occurs when two cats with a close filial relationship, like siblings, mate and produce offspring. Typically this results in genetic flaws that become more serious the deeper the inbreeding penetrates into the gene pool.

Instinct – Instincts are patterns of behavior that are innate and come in automatic response to triggering stimuli in the environment.

Intact - Animals with complete reproductive systems are said to be intact because they are still capable of producing offspring.

J

Jacobsen's Organ – In cats the Jacobsen's Organ is found just behind the upper front teeth on the roof of the mouth. It is comprised of two small openings that function as second nostrils that allow the cat to "taste" odors or scents.

K

Kindle – Kindle is a collective term that refers to a group of cats in one place at one time. Another word with the same meaning is "chowder".

Kitten – A cat is said to be a kitten when it is less than six months of age.

L

Lactation – Lactation is the physical process by which mammary glands produce and secrete milk for the nourishment of young mammals.

Litter – Litter is the collective term for all kittens born at one time to a single mother. Typically this is 3-4, but some litters can be as large as 6-10 or even 12-14 in some breeds.

Litter Box – Litter boxes are really any container of any configuration that is used for the express purpose of providing an indoor cat with a sanitary location to urinate and defecate in a provided collecting material like clay gravel or fine clumping sand.

Longhair – Longhair is a descriptive term for the coat of a cat that is marked by flowing length of fur, plumed tails and neck ruffs.

M

Mites - Small arachnids (*Acarina*) are parasites that infest both animals and plants and are often found in the ear canals of felines.

Moggy – Moggy is a term in the United Kingdom for a mixed breed cat.

Muzzle – A cat's muzzle is that part of the head that projects forward and includes the mouth, jaws and nose. It may alternately be referred to as the snout.

N

Neuter – Neuter is a term that specifically refers to the castration of a male cat to prevent the animal from impregnating females.

Nictitating Membrane – The nictating membrane, or third eyelid, on a cat is an inner transparent eyelid that works to moisten and protect the eye.

Nocturnal – Animals that are nocturnal are most active during the night. This term is mistakenly applied to cats. Felines are actually crepuscular, meaning they are most active at dawn and dusk.

O

Odd-Eyed – When a cat is "odd-eyed" it has two eyes of different colors.

P

Papers – A cat's "papers" are the official documentation of the animal's registered pedigree verifying the authenticity of its lineage as part of a designated breed.

Pedigree - A pedigree is essentially a cat's family tree or genealogy set in writing and covering three or more generations. The record is used to clearly establish the animal's genetic authenticity within a specific breed.

Pet Quality – Purebred cats that are designated to be "pet quality" have some physical characteristic or characteristics that diverge sufficiently from the accepted standard for the breed that they are not considered candidates to be shown or to be used in a breeding program.

Q

Queen – A female cat with an intact reproductive system is called a queen.

Quick – The quick of a cat's claw is the vascular "pink" just behind the white nail that will bleed profusely if it is accidentally clipped.

R

Rabies – Rabies is a highly infectious viral disease typically fatal to warm-blooded animals. It is transmitted by a bite from an infected individual and attacks the central nervous system causing severely aggressive behavior.

Registered Name - The registered name of a cat is the official name used by the registering agency on the animal's pedigree. The name is typically long and contains multiple references to the ancestry of the individual.

S

Scratching Post - A scratching "post" is any structure covered in carpet, rope, or similar material that has been constructed for the express purpose of allowing a domestic cat to sharpen and clean its claws without being destructive to household furnishings.

Shelter – A shelter is any local or regional organization that works to rescue and care for stray, homeless animals with the end goal of placing them in permanent homes.

Show Quality – Show quality cats are individuals that meet the official breed standard for their type and are thus recognized as suitable to be exhibited in cat shows and to be used in breeding programs.

Sire – In a breeding pair of cats, the sire is the male member.

Spay – Spaying is the procedure whereby the ovaries of a female cat are removed to render the animal incapable of producing offspring.

Spray – Spraying is territorial behavior most typically present in male cats involving the emissions of a stream of pungent urine to serve as a territorial marker.

Stud – Studs are male cats that have intact testicles so that they are suitable to serve as half of a mating pair in a breeding program.

T

Tapetum Lucidum - The tapetum lucidum is the interior portion of the feline eye that is highly reflective and aids in night vision. This is the portion of the eye that glows in photographs taken with a flash.

V

Vaccine - A vaccine is a preparation of a weakened or dead pathogen like a bacterium or virus. The vaccine is used to stimulate antibody production for the purpose of creating immunity against disease.

W

Wean – Weaning is the point at which a mother cat breaks her kittens away from subsisting on the milk she produces so that they begin to draw their primary nutrition from solid food.

Whisker Pad - The whisker pad is the thickened area on either side of a cat's face where the animal's sensory whiskers are anchored.

Whole – A whole cat is an individual of either gender with a functioning reproductive system.

References

The Complete Cat Breed Book. DK. April 2013.

Helgren, J. Anne. Encyclopedia of Cat Breeds. Barron's Educational Series, April 2013.

Helgren, J. Anne. Rex Cats (Barron's Complete Pet Owner's Manuals. Barron's Educational Series, January 2001.

King, Chelsea. Devon Rex Cat. Interpet Publishing. June 2003.

Richards, James. ASPCA Complete Guide to Cats: Everything You Need to Know About Choosing and Caring for Your Pet. Chronicle Books. September, 1999.

Rixon, Angela. The Illustrated Encyclopedia of Cat Breeds. Wellfleet Press, January 2011

Photographs

Cover Design:- Liliana Gonzalez Garcia, (info@ipublicidades.com)

Photo by Sonja Pauen Stanhopea
http://commons.wikimedia.org/wiki/File%3AWavy_fur_of_a_Devon_Rex_cat.jpg

Photo by Cojanne
http://commons.wikimedia.org/wiki/File%3APipi_the_red_cat_(female%2C_Devon_Rex_breed)_in_a_box.jpg

Photo by Weimar Meneses
http://commons.wikimedia.org/wiki/File%3ADevon_Rex_-_Weimar_Meneses_(6828524650).jpg

Photo by Bebopscrx

http://commons.wikimedia.org/wiki/File%3ADevon_rex.jpg

Photo by Anthony Ivanoff

http://commons.wikimedia.org/wiki/File%3ADevon_Rex_male.jpg

Photo by Freestyle nl

http://commons.wikimedia.org/wiki/File%3ADevonrex_cat.jpg

All other photographs : www.bigstockphoto.com

Index

A

adoption 16, 17, 18, 25, 28, 29, 133
American Association of Cat Enthusiasts 109
American Cat Fanciers Association 109
arylsulfatase B 82
Australia Cat Federation 109

B

behavior/behaviors 19, 36, 53, 65, 71, 72, 134, 135, 156, 160, 163, 164
boarder 60
bone marrow transplant 82
breeder's association 100
Breeders 17, 20, 24, 97, 98, 100, 133, 136
breeding 24, 96, 98, 99, 101, 102, 103, 109, 154, 155, 162, 163, 164
brushing 64, 73, 159

C

carnivores 39, 71
Cat Fanciers Association 109
cat shows 98, 105, 107, 108, 109, 133, 154, 163
cattery 15, 17, 19, 21, 25, 26, 49, 96, 97, 98, 99, 100, 101, 102, 104, 108, 155

D

declawing 25, 156
diabetes 40, 66
diet 27, 42, 45, 46, 59, 63, 95, 133
disease/diseases 21, 41, 57, 61, 78, 106, 159, 160, 163, 164
distemper combo 77
dry food 39, 44, 125

E

F

G

H

K

L

M

V

W

Notes:

Lightning Source UK Ltd.
Milton Keynes UK
UKHW021343310321
381313UK00008B/1557